DISC[illegible]

The information provided [illegible] is based on the author's experience and res[illegible] and does not guarantee investment advice or trading success. Readers should trade at their own discretion and responsibility.

Trading involves risks, including the potential loss of principal and other losses. When using the content of this book as a reference, it is recommended to also seek advice from investment advisors or professionals.

The author and publisher are not responsible for any losses or damages resulting from actions taken based on the content of this book.

INTRODUCTION

To succeed in the world of trading, merely having excellent strategies and techniques is not enough. A strong mental foundation is essential for consistently making profits in the market. A trader's psychological state directly influences their decisions and actions, ultimately determining the outcomes of their trades.

This book provides guidelines for creating the best mental state for a trader. Based on my own experiences and insights, I systematically explain the psychological skills and mindset necessary for trading.

First, Chapter One outlines what is required for a trader to succeed and the important aspects to achieve it. Next, in Chapter Two, I explain the correct thinking and understanding that traders should acquire. The correct understanding as a trader builds your consistency. In Chapter Three, I address questions I have received and common doubts traders might have. I present how professional traders think and how you should think and act in a Q&A format.

Through these chapters, I aim to clarify what you need to do as a trader, equip you with the necessary skills, and help you gain a deep understanding to embark on your journey as a trader.

My goal with this book is to help readers improve their psychological approach to trading, leading to better decision-making. By practicing the knowledge and techniques provided in this book, you will build mental strength as a trader and achieve long-term success in the market.

The key to surviving in the world of trading is maintaining the right psychological state. This state is achieved through a deep understanding of trading, thought processes, and appropriate belief systems.

I hope this book will serve as a valuable guide in your trading life.

TABLE OF CONTENTS

- Q. When should I adjust my system during real trading?
- Q. Isn't backtesting dangerous because it allows for curve fitting?
- Q. How can I avoid overtrading?
- Q. How important do you think intuition is in trading?
- Q. I'm too busy with work to find time for backtesting.
- Q. What percentage should I set as my daily profit target?
- Q. How do you incorporate news and event risks into your strategy?
- Q. How do you manage drawdowns?
- Q. How should I adjust position sizes in highly volatile markets?
- Q. How much backtesting should I do?
- Q. How should you trade in difficult markets?
- Q. I can't make money because I have little capital.

Conclusion

CHAPTER 1: BUILDING AN EXCELLENT TRADER

In this chapter, we will explain the elements that make up an excellent trader and introduce practical methods to effectively acquire them.
We will introduce various aspects, but each is interconnected and forms the thought processes, beliefs, and habits of a successful trader.
Instead of selectively picking what you find useful or only using parts of it, please try everything.

Even if you attempt to adopt the actions based on probabilistic thinking introduced later, if you do not stop the contradictory actions you have habitually been doing, they will conflict with each other, and you will not be able to successfully acquire new methods.
When learning something new, it is important not to be selective but to try everything exactly as it is.
Please try to incorporate everything I introduce here.
Since all of these are permeated by the core of my thought processes and beliefs, adopting everything rather than partially will more certainly and quickly help you acquire

them.

WHY MANY PEOPLE FAIL TO SUCCEED IN TRADING

Why can't we succeed in trading?
By exploring this secret, we can see "how to succeed."

The world of the market is full of uncertainty, and short-term results are random.
In the short term, even the best strategies can lose, and even the most random trades can win.
Therefore, we do not aim to predict short-term wins and losses, but instead utilize probabilities.
To explain simply, imagine a coin toss where, due to differences in mass and design, the probability of landing heads is biased to 65%.
You don't need to predict whether the next result will be heads or tails.
You just need to keep saying "heads."
This is applied to trading.
This is probabilistic thinking.

However, we still cannot succeed in trading.
This is because there are two problems.

1. Emotional Issues
2. The Perceived Time Frame

Many people are happy when they win.
They are sad when they lose.
This is because they think winning is good and losing is bad.
Since almost everyone starts trading to make money, they hold this belief from the beginning.
This belief always classifies short-term wins and losses as "good" or "bad," creating corresponding emotions.
This makes trading in an uncertain world extremely difficult.
Making decisions based on these "good" and "bad" emotions leads to being swayed by random results.
People reflect on things they shouldn't and celebrate things that are wrong in response to random events.
This hinders consistency.
Many people, no matter how excellent their system is, lose consistency during unavoidable losing streaks or drawdowns, tweak their excellent system, or abandon it halfway, never fully realizing its edge.
Since everyone starts trading to make money, they enter the market with beliefs that make them prone to losses.

Additionally, the time frame we perceive is not half a year or a year, but immediate actions and immediate trading results.
Seeing things from this short focal length causes us to be swayed by randomness.
Probabilities work very slowly, beyond the focal length we can perceive, so it becomes important to place ourselves in a time frame where probabilities work.

From these reasons, you might have a glimpse of why everyone doing trading cannot win.

Now, let's see how we can win in trading, assuming these problems don't exist.

WHAT IT MEANS TO WIN IN TRADING

When most people say they want to win in trading, they are referring to the outcomes of individual trades.
However, this world is one of uncertainty, and short-term results are random.
No matter how perfect your entry is, you can still lose, and no matter how haphazard your entry is, you can still win.
Trying to win against these random events is extremely difficult because it is beyond your control.
However, even though short-term results are random, if you can utilize probabilities, long-term results will no longer be random.
It is important for us to move from the game of winning and losing to the game of probabilities.

To explain briefly, imagine a coin toss where, due to some design or mass difference, the probability of landing heads is 60%.
To win at this coin toss, you just need to keep saying "heads".
You don't need to guess that the next one will be tails because it's "due".
By consistently saying heads, in a short series of 10 tosses, tails might come up more often, or heads might come up 8 times.

This is influenced by randomness.
However, the more times you toss, such as 100 or 1000 times, the less impact randomness has, and the results converge to the actual probability.
This is called the law of large numbers.
We traders also use the law of large numbers to escape the influence of short-term randomness and to draw out our true edge.

This is what it means to win in trading.
It is not about ending each individual trade in profit.
Your job is to always keep saying "heads".

What you need here are:
1. A coin that tends to land heads more often.
2. Consistency in always saying heads.
3. Money management that allows you to repeat the process many times.

These are the essentials for trading.

How does this sound?
What you really need to do is likely very different from what most traders think.
Many people mistakenly believe that winning in trading means winning each individual trade.
From this perspective, they start making efforts to predict each coin toss, which leads to attempting the impossible.
Irrational money management and inconsistent actions, with emotions swayed by the outcomes of individual trades, stem from a fundamental misunderstanding of what it means to win in trading.

With a correct understanding of what it means to win in

trading, proceed to the next page.
We will explain how to achieve these three essential aspects.

THE IMPORTANCE OF A TRADING SYSTEM

To win in trading, consistency is necessary.
By consistently saying "heads," you can make the law of large numbers work in your favor, allowing you to achieve consistent results beyond the influence of short-term randomness.
However, it is crucial to ensure that heads actually has a higher probability of appearing.
This method only works if heads is more likely to appear.
Alternatively, even if the probability of heads is 50%, if the payout is 150% for heads and 100% for tails, it is still important to keep saying "heads."
A trading system is essential to adopting this kind of mechanism in trading.

This is called the edge of the system.
An edge is a positive bias and can also be described as having an advantage.
We find biases, systematize them into rules, and continue to bet on these biases, allowing the law of large numbers to work and generate consistent profits.

At this point, the bias can come from either the system or the behavior.

If the system creates the bias, it is necessary to maintain consistent behavior and let the system's bias work without interference.
On the other hand, if there is no system, positive biases must be created through behavior.
This is discretionary trading that generates profits.
However, I recommend trading systematically rather than discretionarily.
This is because generating positive biases through behavior is very difficult.

Since we start trading to make money, everyone initially holds the belief that "winning is good, losing is bad."
Judging wins and losses as good or bad based on this belief inevitably leads to being affected by short-term randomness.
Seeking to win and trying to avoid losses makes winning very difficult.
As a result, many people cannot win.
A common pattern among those who cannot win is securing profits at small amounts, not cutting losses, and averaging down.
This is behavior driven by the belief that winning is good and losing is bad.
This behavior means continuously using a strategy with a very poor risk-reward ratio.
The more you engage in this behavior, the more the law of large numbers works against you, ensuring that you cannot win.
This is because the belief that you want to make money and avoid losses creates negative biases in your behavior.

Therefore, winning in discretionary trading is very difficult and is a high-difficulty path for most people who start trading to make money.

It is easier to prepare a system with positive biases in advance and follow it consistently, no matter what, allowing the law of large numbers to work.
What is needed here is for you to keep saying "heads."
And your responsibility is to keep saying "heads," not to win.
The challenge is to truly understand this.

WHAT KIND OF SYSTEM IS GOOD

A trading system and strategy should have the following attributes:

- Edge (demonstrated effectiveness through testing with a large number of trials)
- High reproducibility
- Simplicity
- Includes risk management (money management based on the system's performance with a 0% risk of ruin)
- Rules are defined for all situations, leaving no room for ego
- Strictness of rules combined with flexibility to adapt to the market (achievable together)
- Adheres to market principles and is universal (rooted in the mechanics of trends, etc.)
- Not only tells you what to do but also what not to do

Edge:
Without this, you cannot start.
This is a positive bias.
The more you repeat this, the more you will end up with a profit, despite wins and losses along the way.
This balance is struck between risk-reward and win rate.

Risk-reward is the ratio of risk to reward.

If you gain $200 when you win and lose $100 when you lose, the risk-reward ratio is 1:2.
The risk-reward ratio can be expressed as 2 or as 1:2.
The expression may vary, but the meaning is the same.

The performance of the strategy is determined by the win rate of the risk-reward strategy.
For example, even if the risk-reward ratio is 1, if the win rate is 65%, there is an edge.
On the other hand, even if the risk-reward ratio is 2, if the win rate is 20%, there is no edge.
The more you repeat it, the more your capital will decrease.

Thus, it is not enough for the risk-reward ratio to be good; the win rate must also be good.
You need a strategy that balances these to create an edge.

High reproducibility:
A system with too many variables and difficult to replicate is not good.
It should be easy to understand and follow instructions.
For example, if you use too many indicators or the rules are too complex, each indicator may give conflicting signals, making it difficult to decide which rule to follow, leading to the inability to replicate the system accurately.
A simple, easy-to-follow system is desirable.
Without high reproducibility, it becomes difficult to collect trade samples under the same conditions, and the edge drawn out may differ significantly from what was tested.
Ideally, the rules should be simple, clear, strict, and flexible enough to adapt to the market.
These can coexist.

Includes risk management:

When creating a system, it is important to include risk management in the rules.
This is because risk management needs to be specific to that system.
Since the performance of each system differs, risk management should be tailored to the system's performance.
For example, even if a book states that the risk per trade should be 3%, if it does not match your system's performance, you should not use it.
You must adopt a risk management approach that ensures 0% risk of ruin, allowing for safe and stable long-term operation based on your system's performance.
The system assumes repetition.
Losing streaks and drawdowns are unavoidable.
Therefore, do not trade with a position size that would cause catastrophic damage from a 5 or 10 losing streak.

Rules that cover all situations leaving no room for ego:
Rules should not only define where to buy and where to close positions but also cover responses to economic events, how far in advance you can enter, or whether you should trade that day at all.
If not predetermined, emotional decisions might take over.
You should not decide to trade for reasons unrelated to trading, such as wanting to recover from a loss or having not traded recently.
Additionally, each trader handling the system has their personality and behavioral quirks.
Creating rules for trading and beyond that suit the person is also important.
For example, don't look at charts at certain times, don't trade if you're unsure, or trade everything if you're unsure,

don't trade if you're feeling rushed, don't trade if you can't concentrate, etc.
Our job is to collect quality trade samples over time, and trading in a rushed state or when unable to concentrate leads to poor quality trade samples.
Choosing not to trade in such cases is also important.
Not trading will not contaminate the quality of the trade samples, but chasing trades in a rushed state will degrade their quality.
It is necessary to decide on rules that respond to your psychological state in advance.
This is important to understand your behavioral patterns and personality through tools like trading journals.

Systems that adhere to market principles and are universal:
A system based on the mechanisms of trends or market principles will not become obsolete.
The ideal is to study the market and build a system while forming hypotheses during that process.
If you use a system that contradicts your understanding of the market, it will be difficult to follow its instructions honestly, and if it does not follow market mechanisms, it may work temporarily but eventually become unusable.

Tells you what not to do, as well as what to do:
It is important for a system to tell you not only when to trade but also when not to trade.
In my case, I understand the market on multiple time frames, and the entry and exit rules are on the 1-hour chart, but I don't trade unless the market environment on the 4-hour or daily chart is aligned.
It is necessary to know the market environment in which the entry signal will work in advance.

THE IMPORTANCE OF BACKTESTING

Whether you are creating a system or testing it, backtesting is very important.
By conducting thorough backtesting, you can gain a deep understanding of the system and build trust in it.
Without knowing the system's performance, you won't know the appropriate position size, nor will you understand the potential drawdowns or losing streaks, leaving you constantly anxious.
Constant anxiety over random outcomes makes it difficult to consistently use the system and draw out its edge.

Using an untested system is itself a risk and should be considered gambling.
Many people tend to avoid the tedious task of backtesting, but using a system you don't understand is never beneficial.
Even if it's tedious, make sure to conduct thorough testing.

Reasons to Perform Backtesting:
- To confirm the system has an edge
- To build a system with an edge
- To identify and manage risks
- To practice recognizing signals from charts and acting accordingly, thereby gaining confidence

- To clearly define rules to eliminate any room for ego
- To eliminate emotional decisions
- Using an untested system is a risk and gambling
- Not using a system leads to inconsistent trading, unclear edge extraction, and being constantly swayed by immediate results, increasing the difficulty of trading
- While some compare it to forward testing, both are important. It's unrealistic to forward test for 10 years, but backtesting allows efficient testing.

Backtesting should not only be done to gather data but also to practice in a way that simulates real scenarios.
In backtesting, it's easy to fast-forward time, leading to carelessness, but you should practice with the mindset of anticipating the next scenario and patiently waiting for the plan to unfold.
As with any sport or activity, practice mimics the actual performance.
Although practice is different from actual performance, its effectiveness changes based on what the practitioner anticipates and imagines.
By conducting backtesting with the mindset of real trading, planning meticulously, it will prove highly beneficial in actual trading.

The number of backtests should be as large as possible.
A larger sample size increases reliability statistically.
If you perform a few tests or only over specific periods, reliability decreases, leading to lower confidence in the system, increased anxiety during drawdowns, and a higher risk of tweaking or abandoning the system prematurely.

First, conduct 100 backtests to roughly determine if there is

an edge.
With a good risk-reward ratio and win rate, you can identify an edge even with about 100 tests.
If an edge is present, conduct at least another 1000 backtests to measure more detailed performance.
100 tests are too few statistically and do not provide a reliable sample size to understand the true performance of the system.
Real trading with few tests will inevitably encounter unexperienced events, creating anxiety and misunderstanding about the system's functionality, leading to inconsistency.
Moreover, it might turn out that the system didn't have an edge in the first place.
Although it may seem tedious, conduct backtesting with a large sample size.
This provides accurate performance metrics, allowing for risk-free money management based on maximum drawdowns and losing streaks.

I always perform over 1000 backtests.
From my perspective, 1000 tests don't seem like a lot.
If you work seriously every day, you can achieve 1000 tests in a few days.

In addition to this, I constantly perform backtests as practice, resulting in an enormous amount of backtesting over time.
It is possible to achieve 10,000 backtests in 1-2 months of daily dedicated effort.
Considering I have been doing this daily for years as practice, I have likely conducted hundreds of thousands to millions of backtests without exaggeration.
I take pride in having done more backtests than anyone else,

but backtesting never betrays.
It always supports your confidence, discipline, and consistency.

FORWARD TESTING

Once you have conducted thorough backtesting, the next step is forward testing.
Please adhere to this order.
Always forward test what you have backtested.
It takes too much time and is highly inefficient to forward test without knowing if the system has an edge.
Many people compare forward testing and backtesting, but both are important.
They have completely different roles.
It is unrealistic to forward test for ten years, but backtesting can efficiently test this.
You need to test whether you can consistently execute what you tested on a large amount of data in real-time.
Therefore, being anxious about whether there is an edge at the stage of forward testing adds an extra burden.
To repeat, always conduct forward testing with a backtested system.

In forward testing, test whether the capital increases consistently over about three months and whether you can act according to the rules.
For me, it's three months, but this is up to you.
However, it is desirable to do it for at least a month.

Use a demo account or a very small account for this.

After experiencing a major failure once, I created a rule not to engage in real trading until I had increased capital stably for three months in a demo account, thus not exposing actual capital to risk.
I feel this saved me a lot of money.
Do not rush.
If you have the skills, the money will follow.
If you lose your valuable money before acquiring the skills, it's over.

If there are no problems with forward testing, it's time for the real deal.

REAL TRADING

After thoroughly completing backtesting and forward testing, your task in real trading is to maintain discipline and consistently repeat your trades.
You need to identify what disrupts your consistency and correct any faulty thought processes or beliefs.
Focus on maintaining consistency above all else, without thinking about how much money you have made.

The main content of this book is to help you acquire consistency to maximize your abilities as a trader.
Therefore, if your preparation so far is insufficient, go back to backtesting and thoroughly prepare yourself.

In real trading, you should monitor yourself and keep records.
Since you only need to follow the rules, there is no need to worry about various things in real trading.
If you find yourself worrying, record that as well.
I repeat, there should be no ambiguity or uncertainty in the rules during real trading. If there is, go back and thoroughly perform backtesting and forward testing.

Investigate why you cannot adhere to clear rules, why you are tempted to act against them, and what is trying to disrupt your consistency.
This is the beginning of your journey as a trader.
The trade journal becomes crucial here.

The trade journal is extremely important, so make sure to keep one.

TRADE JOURNAL

The Importance and Optimal Use of a Trade Journal

A trade journal is a powerful tool for personal growth and strategy improvement, beyond just recording trades.
Many traders tend to neglect this habit, but its value is immeasurable.
The journal is a place to write down details about trades, thoughts, emotions, and challenges faced.
This makes it easier to look back on the past and provides opportunities to notice immature judgments and mistakes.
Many people think a trade journal is unnecessary, but you can't reflect without something to review.
Your problems are unique to you and manifest in your actions and thoughts.
Recording these as material for reflection is crucial for improvement.

What you should record:
- Records of trades, screenshots
- Thoughts and emotions
- All actions related to trading
- Learnings about trading
- Articles about thought processes and beliefs you want to develop

Write these in your trade journal.

I will explain them in order.

Records of trades, screenshots:
Always take screenshots of the trades you make.
The most important are the screenshots just before the trade and right after the entry.
Many people may take screenshots after the trade, but what's more important are the ones before and right after the entry.
The reasons are:
- To avoid outcome bias
- To determine if the entry was appropriate according to the rules
- To foster a sense of collecting samples of correct entries
For these reasons.

If you only journal after trades, you will unknowingly accumulate a lot of journals biased by the outcomes.
The process is more important than the results.
Regardless of whether you win or lose, you must judge if it was a trade worth making without being influenced by the results.
Collecting a large number of screenshots before knowing the results makes it easier to get a sense of collecting "things," helping you feel like you are making the trades you should.
This nurtures a trader's crucial sense of collecting trade samples without being attached to the outcomes.

Thoughts and emotions:
Also, write your thoughts and emotions in the trade journal.
This information is valuable not only after the trade but also before the trade and while waiting for a trade, times when you are not influenced by outcome bias.
I recommend developing a habit of writing whenever you

think or feel something.

By writing down your thoughts and emotions, you can identify the beliefs and thought processes you hold.
Your beliefs hinder consistency.
Emotions appear according to your beliefs and thought processes, so conversely, when emotions appear, it means some belief or thought process is at work.
Identifying this allows you to transform from faulty thought processes to correct ones.

All actions related to trading:
You unconsciously take actions driven by your beliefs.
These may be habits you don't notice yourself.
For example, if you believe "winning is good, losing is bad," you will go to great lengths to avoid losing.
Even if you understand the importance of probabilistic thinking, this faulty belief will generate strong feelings of aversion to immediate losses, prompting actions based on those feelings.
You might constantly check the chart during a trade or be overly concerned with the movement of your profits and losses.
Thinking about boasting on social media when you win also stems from this faulty belief.
When this behavior becomes habitual or stronger, winning becomes tied to self-esteem, making trading extremely dangerous.
In this state, you will absolutely not want to lose, making it very difficult to maintain consistency.
Before reaching this point, it is crucial to record and closely observe your actions, experimenting to avoid such behaviors.

Learnings about trading:
Write down anything you learn about trading.
Not just about charts, but also important thoughts and influences.

You may encounter wonderful ideas or words in books or on social media.
At that point, they are still someone else's words, not yours.
There is a big difference between understanding something and turning it into your own words through your thought process.
Write down important thoughts and words repeatedly to make them your own.
When you encounter words that resonate with you, write them down and construct sentences leading to that conclusion repeatedly.
Continue writing until your thought process naturally reaches that conclusion.
This is not just about memorizing things but about training your thought process through repetition. It is important to write repeatedly, not just once.
Your expressions and phrasing may change each time, but that's okay.
Just continue to weave your own words towards the same conclusion repeatedly.

Always write these things.
To face yourself, having records of yourself is essential.
You might think you know yourself well enough not to write things down, but surprisingly, you don't.
Your unconscious actions are literally unconscious, so to consciously recognize them, you need to present them in a

visible form.
The trade journal is not just a record but an important training ground for forming your thought processes.
It is crucial to use the trade journal to its fullest, so make it a daily habit.

As you continue these practices, your patterns will emerge.
You might think you are taking different actions each time, but you are following the same patterns.
Your areas for improvement will become apparent from these patterns.
This is not only useful for your actions but also for improving your system.
Losses appearing in the same patterns become easier to address.
Once a system is established, it should not be altered lightly.
Systems are balanced delicately, and even minor changes can greatly impact performance.
If changes are made, backtesting must be done from scratch.
These changes should not be influenced by randomness.
Thus, any modifications or improvements should be based on statistical evidence.
Only address losses that form consistent patterns; treat everything else as random outcomes.
The more passionate you are, the more you may want to make immediate improvements with each loss, but refrain from doing so.
Primarily, these adjustments should be made during backtesting or forward testing, and in real trading, your focus and improvements should be on maintaining your consistency.

THE DOOR TO DISCIPLINE AND CONSISTENCY

Once you have thoroughly prepared, the next step is to focus on maintaining discipline and consistency in real trading.
No matter how excellent your system is, losing streaks and drawdowns are unavoidable.
Your discipline and consistency will constantly be tested.
In other words, your skill as a trader is determined by your discipline and consistency.

The main theme of this book is discipline and consistency.
This is the essence of a trader's skill.

To maintain a high level of discipline and consistency, there are things you must deeply understand.

1. A true understanding of a trader's job
2. Mastering the edge and reproducibility skills through thorough backtesting and practice
3. Understanding and embodying probabilistic thinking through actions
4. Understanding how probability works

It is crucial to integrate these as a single, cohesive approach through your actions.

Discipline and consistency are inherently very simple and easy.
In trading, it's just about waiting and clicking.
However, it becomes difficult because of the belief that "winning is good, losing is bad."
This stems from the desire to make money, a belief held by almost all traders from the beginning.
Moreover, even without money involved, there is the belief that "winning and losing are tied to self-worth," which leads to an aversion to losing, mistaking it as a denial of oneself.
Some people strongly exhibit this tendency even when trading on a demo account where no money is involved.

Those who don't trade might think that "waiting and clicking" sounds very simple, but only those who trade understand how difficult it is.
And the level of skill required for this simple repetition of "waiting and clicking" is beyond imagination.
Mastering this skill may be more about eliminating what hinders it rather than gaining something.

After learning the four principles mentioned earlier, the next phase is to "deeply" understand them.
This is the phase where you eliminate what has a negative impact.
To deeply understand what you have learned and embody it through actions, you must discard your previous habits and thought processes.
Learning is relatively easy, but this phase of discarding is extremely challenging.

So, let's go through this step by step.

① A TRUE UNDERSTANDING OF A TRADER'S JOB

A trader's work involves two modes.
I call them the Boss Mode and the Employee Mode.
In Boss Mode, you develop strategies based on long-term perspectives and statistical data, and refine these through trial and error into practical rules.
In Employee Mode, you execute the orders given by the boss faithfully.

You, as a single individual, must operate in both of these modes, but not at the same time.
For example, the work done in Boss Mode should be outside trading hours, not during trading.
On the other hand, when in Employee Mode, you must follow the company's rules no matter what, just like an employee cannot arbitrarily start a bargain sale because there are few customers or change the price tags to make up for losses, or gamble the company's money.
An employee who doesn't follow the rules becomes a risk and will be dismissed.
Your job is to follow the instructions and not worry about

daily sales figures; that's for the boss to consider from a long-term perspective.

In trading, the work done in Boss Mode involves developing strategies, thoroughly testing them, confirming their statistical functionality, and creating a system with practical rules.
Learning about the market, backtesting, and forward testing are tasks for you in Boss Mode.
The key is how thoroughly you, in Boss Mode, can prepare so that you, in Employee Mode, can act appropriately without hesitation.

In Employee Mode, it is crucial to follow the discipline and instructions no matter what.
You don't need to worry about recovering your wages if there are few customers.

In trading, it is very important to distinguish between these two modes.
Especially in actual trading, you are in Employee Mode.
If you don't properly recognize your job and role, you might ignore the instructions you should follow and start making your own improvements.
This leads to a lack of consistency.

No matter how excellent the system, losing streaks and drawdowns caused by randomness are unavoidable.
These losing streaks and drawdowns appear to have patterns, but they actually don't, and they can't be conquered by direct involvement.
Therefore, we must trust the results of extensive pre-testing and act without being swayed by the outcomes.
It is contradictory to try to leverage a statistical edge but be

swayed by immediate results.
Even if you face a losing streak, your next action remains the same.
You must not change it.

By thinking in terms of these two modes, you can focus on the tasks at hand and identify where the problems lie in your work.
Once your role and tasks are clear, you just need to focus on the assigned work without thinking about anything else.

The work in Boss Mode should be done outside trading hours, and the key is how thoroughly you can engage in it.
There is a lot of tedious preliminary work, and it's easy to slack off depending on your personality, but if you do, the employee will lose trust in the boss's work and will not follow instructions easily.
The majority of trading work is done in the preparation stage, so make sure to do it thoroughly.

In Employee Mode, it's all about how well you can follow the instructions.
All the problems in the actual market arise in this mode, so the key is how much you can avoid focusing on immediate results and concentrate only on the given instructions.

Understanding the work of a trader based on this will be crucial.
Knowing how much you understand and what your current scope of responsibility is will allow you to perform the best in your role without unnecessary worries.

The work of a trader is to accurately become and function as a part of the system to bring out the system's edge.

In Boss Mode, you prepare a system with an edge, and in Employee Mode, you demonstrate discipline and consistency.
In Employee Mode, your only responsibility is to follow the rules, and you are not responsible for the results.
Your responsibility is to follow the rules strictly, and you must not do anything else.
Remember firmly that you must not do anything else.
Regardless of losing, streaks, or drawdowns, you must not do anything outside the instructions.
The market will test your discipline and consistency with all sorts of events.
No matter what happens, stick to your plan.
Against unavoidable losing streaks and drawdowns, our response is not to try to avoid them but to trust and continue repeating the same thing no matter what.

Always be aware of which mode you are working in now.

COLUMN

What is necessary to make trading boring:

You are not bored with trading yet.
Even though you have a system and rules in place, you are always afraid, always happy or sad.
Most people are happy when they win.
They are sad when they lose.
This is because they believe that winning is good and losing is bad.

Almost everyone starts trading because they want to make money, so they have this belief from the beginning.
This belief always classifies the immediate wins and losses as "good" or "bad" and generates corresponding emotions.
This makes trading in a world of uncertainty incredibly difficult.
If you make judgments based on these feelings of "good" and "bad," you will be swayed by random results.
You will reflect on things that you don't need to reflect on for random events, and you will be happy about things that are wrong.
This interferes with consistency.

No matter how excellent a system many people have, they lose consistency due to inevitable losing streaks and drawdowns, tinker with excellent systems, or abandon them halfway through, judging them to be unusable, and are never able to draw out the edge.

Since everyone starts trading because they want to make money, it means that everyone is participating in the market with a belief that makes them prone to losing.

Therefore, you yourself are the biggest weakness when it comes to drawing out the edge of the system.

In other words, it is extremely important to change your mistaken beliefs and thought processes.

The following deep understandings play an important role.

- Understand from a probabilistic perspective and do not place value on immediate wins and losses.
- Understand that acting according to the rules, whether winning or losing, or even choosing not to trade, is all earning expected value.
- Understand that your job is to follow the rules and that you are not responsible for wins and losses.
- The way probability works is very slow and not at the focal length you can perceive. Therefore, it makes no sense at all to care about the immediate results.
- Rather than having a long-term perspective, the ideal state is one in which you have completely lost interest in short-term results, and before you know it, months have passed.
- Have a sense of drawing out the edge over a year.
- Understand that if you do anything other than the rules, the system will not function accurately.
- Understand that the quality of the trading sample is important. Vow not to rush or chase trades.

It is important to embody these, not just understand them in your head.
It is easy to read and understand this, but you must embody it in your actions.
To do this, let's stop the behaviors and habits that arise from the mistaken belief of placing value on winning and losing.
- Don't look at charts unnecessarily.
- Don't calculate the amount or position size to make up for losses.
- Don't look at profit and loss during a trade.
- Don't think about bragging when you win.

If you do not stop these behaviors based on mistaken beliefs, it is meaningless to think that probabilistic thinking is important.
This is because your actions are contradictory.

When your actions and understanding are in alignment, your scope of responsibility as a trader becomes clear, your actions become clear, and things become simple and easy.
If you truly understand, you will lose interest in the immediate results, lose interest in your current account balance, and as a result, you will naturally place yourself on the time axis where probability works, and before you know it, several months or half a year will have passed.
Trading in this state is boring.
In this way, you can become the best state as a trader whose job is to make probability work.

② CONFIRMING THE EDGE AND ACQUIRING REPRODUCIBILITY SKILLS THROUGH THOROUGH BACKTESTING AND PRACTICE

You have two modes: Boss Mode and Employee Mode, and it is crucial to perfectly fulfill the roles of each mode, but you, as one individual, perform both.

This means that you, the employee, see how trustworthy the boss is and how well the boss's job is done.

The boss is monitored in all aspects of their work, and this work directly affects the employee's tasks, making the boss's work extremely important.

As the boss, you need to understand the market well, find market biases, form hypotheses, and create a system with an edge by repeatedly backtesting various entry and exit rules.
You don't need to create it from scratch; it can be something taught by someone else or learned from a book, but the most important thing is that you yourself thoroughly backtest it, understand it, and trust it.
Don't think, "Someone else did the backtesting, so I don't need to."
When you use the system, the results come from you using it.
The results you get from using it are different from those someone else would get.
You must always backtest it yourself and know what the results will be when you use the system.
Most importantly, you need to be able to execute the system's rules without missing them, even when faced with an uncertain future chart.
Repeated backtesting also serves as practice for this.
While collecting data, it also serves as practice for operating your system, deepening your understanding and trust in the system.

Understanding and trusting your system are essential to passing the test of discipline and consistency that will inevitably come with losing streaks and drawdowns.
Thorough backtesting will reveal how many consecutive losses are possible, whether a month could end in a loss, and whether, by repeating the process, you can significantly increase your capital by the end of the year.
Knowing these things beforehand makes a significant difference.
Every excellent system will experience losing streaks and

drawdowns, and since you won't know when these will end, how much you trust the system, or how well you "know" it, becomes crucial.

Backtesting is not just about gathering data; it's also important to practice with real-world scenarios in mind.
Since you can fast-forward time in backtesting, it tends to become sloppy, but try to do it carefully with the mindset of anticipating the next scenario and patiently waiting for the plan to unfold.
As with any sport or activity, practice mimics actual performance.
Although practice differs from actual performance, the effect changes based on what the practitioner anticipates and imagines.
If you conduct backtesting with the real trading scenarios in mind and plan carefully, it will undoubtedly be beneficial in actual trading.

People often compare backtesting and forward testing, but they serve completely different roles and should not be compared.
Both are important.
It is unrealistic to forward test for ten years.
However, backtesting can quickly gather ten years' worth of data, allowing for various trial and error within a long period.
Make sure to forward test strategies that have been thoroughly backtested and confirmed to have an edge.
In backtesting, set detailed strategic rules, and in forward testing, set rules to address actions stemming from your own feelings of anxiety or nervousness in real-time scenarios.
Rules should not only be strategic but also include those addressing your own behavior, which could pose risks.

③ UNDERSTANDING PROBABILISTIC THINKING AND EMBODYING IT THROUGH ACTION

A trader's job is to create a system with an edge, accurately operate it to collect a large number of samples, and use the law of large numbers to converge probabilities and bring out the system's edge.
Once you create a system with an edge through backtesting and other methods, you then need to operate it accurately and continuously to collect a large number of samples.

Trading exists in a world of uncertainty.
In a world where the same chart never appears twice, to win, you need to use probabilities.
While the charts never exactly repeat, this is when considering them very precisely.
When you loosen the focus a bit and abstract, similar patterns become visible.
This is because, even if the exact charts do not repeat, the

mechanisms are the same.
Just as history doesn't exactly repeat but learning from it is valuable because human psychological mechanisms remain the same, the same patterns emerge when abstracting charts.
To draw concrete results from these similar patterns, you need to collect many samples of the same pattern to make the silhouette clear.
This is how you use the law of large numbers to draw out the true probability.

We often say to trade with probabilistic thinking, so let's explain probabilistic thinking again briefly.
Suppose you have a coin where, for some reason, the probability of landing heads is 60%, and you participate in a coin toss game.
If you can only play five times, all results could be tails.
But if you play 100, 1000, or 10,000 times, the results will converge to the true probability of 60%.
No matter how many losing streaks you have along the way.
In this coin toss game, your task is not to predict whether the next result will be heads or tails.
Your correct action is always to say "heads."

In trading, unless you decide to retire, you can keep increasing the number of trades.
If you can only trade five times, the law of probability won't work, but with each trade, your sample size will continue to increase.
You need to build all of these samples with "heads."
This is what I mean when I often say "build with only high-quality trade samples."

Quality does not refer to winning or losing.

It means whether you said "heads" in the coin toss.
In other words, it means whether you perfectly followed the instructions of the system with an edge.
Continuing to act according to the rules means collecting high-quality trade samples.
This is what is meant by the importance of discipline and consistency.

You are constantly tested for discipline and consistency through losing streaks and drawdowns.
You must trust your system and the laws of probability.
How well you understand your system and the laws of probability is crucial.

The most important thing is to "embody" this understanding through action.
I will explain how to do this practically later.

④ UNDERSTANDING HOW PROBABILITY WORKS

Even if you understand probabilistic thinking, it is crucial to further understand how probability works.
The key point to grasp is that "probability works much slower than you think."
This is the most important thing to emphasize.

Probability works through the law of large numbers, but "large numbers" refers to very large quantities in reality.
Gathering such large numbers, like 1000, 10000, or 100000, one by one in real-time takes a considerable amount of time.
And the effects of these numbers go beyond our perception.
We cannot recognize when probability is working.
Despite this, the reason why capital increases is due to the performance of the system, based on the risk-reward ratio and win rate.
Many people think that since their capital is increasing, probability must be working, but actually, it is just the performance helping out, not the precise manifestation of the system's edge.
If you perform 100 trades in a year, the results will be quite

varied.
However, even with the variations, the capital is increasing.
As you continue for 5 or 10 years, the sample size grows, stabilizing the capital growth, and the effect of compounding starts to work.

For example, even if you have a system with a risk-reward ratio of 2 and a win rate of 70%, by the 30th trade, your capital might not have increased significantly.
This occurs due to the dispersion of results caused by randomness, but by the 100th trade, the capital should have increased.
However, at the 30th trade, we often feel anxious and think something might be wrong with our method or that the system might not work, leading us to make unnecessary improvements or abandon the system, thus losing consistency.
While 30 trades might feel like a lot to us, it is still a small sample size from the perspective of the law of large numbers.
Therefore, we cannot recognize when probability is working.
The crucial understanding here is that "probability works much slower than you think."
By understanding this beforehand, you can counteract the anxiety felt in real-time.

Understanding your job and scope of responsibility as a trader, trusting and understanding the system, probabilistic thinking, and understanding how probability works are all ultimately necessary to control your own behavior, which is the greatest risk to maintaining discipline and consistency.
The door to consistency can be reached by unifying these understandings and embodying them through your actions.

COLUMN

Learn How Probability Works □

As a trader using probabilities, it is very important to understand how probability works.
I have explained this before, but I will explain it again.
The law of probability works much slower than you might think, and during that time, you need to continue operating your system.
If you do not understand how probability works, many traders will become anxious during periods when it seems like their funds are not increasing, and they will make the mistake of tampering with the system or switching to another method, failing to draw out the edge of their system even though they have a good one.
If you have thoroughly tested in advance, you must continue to follow the rules no matter what.

Today, we want to look at a system with a risk-reward ratio of 2 and a win rate of 70%, which is a fairly good system.
(This is an example. We will examine what happens in the case of a good system.)
Let's look at a simulation of trading 100 times a year with a

risk of 1% per trade.

First, look at this image.

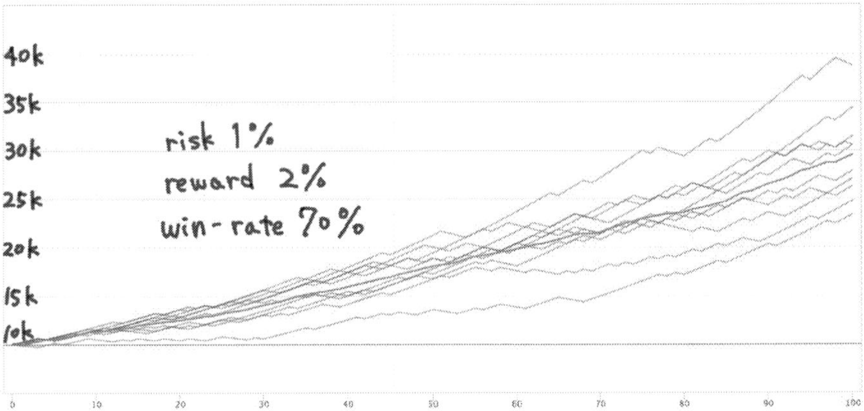

This is a simulation of 10 runs of 100 trials, so there are 10 graphs.
With a small number of trials, like 100, the results will vary between good and bad times.

Looking only at this result, you might think, "I want to use this system if it can make this much money," but I want you to pay attention to the interim results.
The next attached image is the graph at the 30th trial, which had the worst performance.

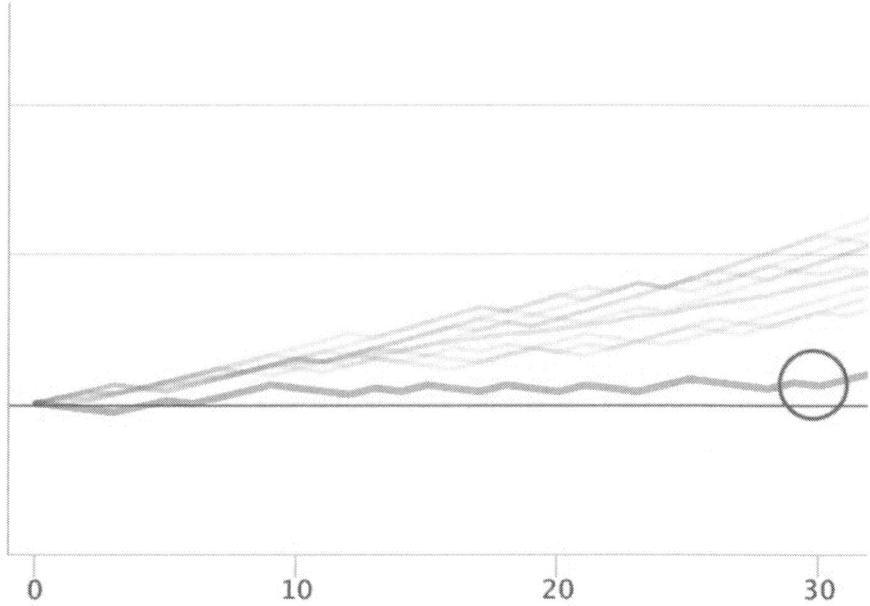

At this point, there is almost no profit, and since you cannot see the right side of the graph at this point, you might feel anxious if this is your performance in the third month of using the system.
However, if you continue to repeat this, the funds will ultimately increase by more than 200%.

Even with such a good system, this is the result with about 30 trials.
This is what randomness is and what probability is.
Can you continue to trade consistently in the same way after 30 trades if you don't know what the right side of the graph looks like?
Can you still trust the statistics?
You might start looking for reasons, thinking that there is something wrong with not seeing an increase in funds for

three months, and try to make improvements or look for another system out of goodwill.
But if you do that, you won't be able to draw out the edge that you could have.
This is one of the reasons why many traders cannot draw out the edge even though they have a good system.
Many traders think that if they have a good system, they will naturally develop consistency and it will be easy to repeat, but that is not the case.

When I always say "probability works much slower than you think," I mean this.
If you do not understand this, it will be very difficult to draw out the edge of the system as a trader.

Key points□
- The edge does not appear within the range we recognize.
- The range we recognize only looks random.
- Looking at things from this focal length will cause you to be swayed by the results and you will not be able to win in trading.
- What you should be looking at within the range we recognize is the process and what you need to do now.
- The result will be there when you realize it.

As a trader, you need to understand that your job is to continue following the system's rules to utilize the law of probability and that probability works much slower than you think.

Not knowing about probability as a trader using the law of probability is the same as not knowing much about your job.
Understanding how probability works is something you need to understand as you work as a trader.

And of course, as a fundamental premise, you must know the edge of your system with a large sample size in advance. Make sure to thoroughly prepare in advance.

EMBODYING PROBABILISTIC THINKING

Merely knowing probabilistic thinking is meaningless.
Even if we understand probabilistic thinking, we cannot win because we do not embody it through our actions.
Embodying it means achieving complete understanding.
We can only act in accordance with our beliefs, and to embody something means it has become a new belief.

For example, if you hold the false belief that "immediate wins and losses are important," you will always judge wins and losses as "good" or "bad," generating emotions accordingly, and you will act according to that belief.
Trying to practice probabilistic thinking while holding the belief that immediate wins and losses are important creates a contradiction.
This is because probability does not prioritize individual results.
Although you may think you are trading with probabilistic thinking, losing streaks or winning streaks will sway you, causing you to make changes under the guise of "improvement" or abandon the system altogether, thus failing

to maintain consistency.

This false belief is something all traders start with since they begin trading out of a desire to earn money.
This is why most traders fail.

This belief manifests in actions driven by emotions, such as:
- Checking the charts frequently for no reason
- Focusing only on profits and losses during trades
- Constantly worrying about account balances
- Feeling joy when winning and anger when losing
- Feeling anxious when there are few trading opportunities
- Feeling jealousy or anxiety when seeing others win

These are just examples, but beliefs manifest in all actions.

Unless you stop these behaviors, even if you think you understand probabilistic thinking, repeating the habits you have developed will continually reinforce the false belief that emphasizes wins and losses.
Without resolving this contradiction, you cannot truly understand probabilistic thinking.

To truly understand probabilistic thinking, you must stop all contradictory behaviors and replace them with actions based on the belief in probabilistic thinking.
Your actions reflect your beliefs.
True understanding of probabilistic thinking means becoming indifferent to results, eliminating actions related to results, focusing on the large number of trials, and ultimately shifting your timeframe to one where probabilities work.
True understanding is not "knowing" as knowledge but "embodying" through actions.
This is the path I have walked, and the reason I repeatedly

emphasize the importance of embodiment is because it is the final form of understanding.

Knowledge is just the initial stage of understanding.
Let's stop all contradictory actions born from the false belief that values results and replace them with actions that embody probabilistic thinking.

STOP ACTING ON FALSE BELIEFS

We start trading because we want to make money.
From the moment we start trading, we have the belief that "winning and increasing our funds is good, and losing and decreasing our funds is bad."
In this uncertain world, short-term results are influenced by randomness.
No matter how correctly you enter, you will lose, and no matter how recklessly you enter, you will win.
If you consider winning to be good and losing to be bad, you will always be swayed by this randomness.
To achieve consistent results in an uncertain world, you must use the law of probability, but probability does not emphasize individual outcomes.
As long as you continue to focus on individual results, you cannot maintain consistency.

The false belief that "winning is good and losing is bad" drives your actions through emotions.
All your unconscious actions and habits are based on some belief.
Identify and stop all actions and habits based on false beliefs.
Here are some examples.
Stop anything that resonates with you.

- Checking charts frequently without reason
- Focusing solely on profits and losses during trades
- Constantly worrying about account balance
- Feeling happy when you win and angry when you lose
- Feeling anxious when trading opportunities are scarce
- Feeling jealous or impatient when seeing others win
- Feeling an urge to check charts even when not looking at them
- Thinking about bragging on social media when you win
- Always thinking based on the highest account balance you've had
- Getting excited when seeing large amounts of money on social media

There may be more, but since there are individual differences, record and face your actions to identify them.
Basically, believe that all actions accompanied by emotions are related to beliefs.

Here are specific examples of how to deal with the examples mentioned above.

- Checking charts frequently without reason
Utilize alarms and chart alerts.
Set alerts to sound when conditions are right for you to check the charts, and do not open the charts otherwise.

- Focusing solely on profits and losses during trades
Remove the display of PL during trades from the charts.
Use such functions available on the platform you use.

- Constantly worrying about account balance
Hide the account balance display.
If you cannot hide it, be careful not to align your gaze with

where the balance is displayed.

- Feeling happy when you win and angry when you lose
Always set a stop loss at entry, and make arrangements so that the settlement will be completed automatically even if you are not looking at the chart.
Even if you receive a settlement notification, do not open the chart immediately and wait for some time.

- Feeling anxious when trading opportunities are scarce
Use alarms and alerts to manage the times when you should check the charts, and spend your time on hobbies unrelated to trading.
Think about the importance of patiently waiting for your trades, no matter how much time it takes.

- Feeling jealous or impatient when seeing others win
Do not look at accounts that only post when they are winning.
Do not look at posts that only show the amount of money earned.
Such posts are of no benefit to you.
Do not look at accounts that post trading content.
If you have determined what you should do, seeing such posts will only pose a risk to you.

- Feeling an urge to check charts even when not looking at them
Find fun hobbies other than trading.
Do things that require concentration.

- Thinking about bragging on social media when you win
Decide not to post your trading results on social media.
Unless you have a special reason, such as explaining your trades to someone, there is no meaning in posting your trades.

It is likely being done to satisfy your ego, so decide not to post such things from the start.

- Always thinking based on the highest account balance you've had
Do not look at the account balance.
Understand that there is no point in looking.
Understand that your brain will automatically react to that information if you look.

- Getting excited when seeing large amounts of money on social media
Avoid looking at posts that display amounts of money.
If they catch your eye, scroll past them before reading the information.

These are just examples.
Try to come up with your own ideas and strategies.
The key is to "not look" and "not display" the sources of the problem.
Our minds automatically start thinking about the things we see.
If you don't see the numbers in the first place, you won't make unnecessary calculations or create suffering based on them.
It's important not to see them from the start.
Even on social media, no matter how mentally stable and in a good mood you are, seeing negative or aggressive posts will make you feel bad.
That is because your mind reacts to that information and automatically starts thinking.
Just as it is effective to mute or avoid seeing negative or aggressive posts on social media, it is effective and easier to avoid seeing information that can pose a risk to your trading.

The rules you decide on "not to do" are very important.
In trading, what you don't do is more important than what you do.
Put all actions based on false beliefs and anything that can pose a risk to your trading on your "not to do list."

TO CONTINUE ROLLING A DICE WITH AN EDGE

1. True Understanding of a Trader's Job
2. Confirmation of Edge and Skill Acquisition through Thorough Backtesting and Practice of the System
3. Understanding and Embodying Probabilistic Thinking
4. Understanding How Probability Works

I explained these four essential elements to become a successful trader.
It is important to connect these into concrete actions.
When these are fully integrated into one understanding and reflected in your actions, it becomes no different from continuously rolling a dice.

Your job as a trader is to prepare a favorable dice through thorough testing and keep rolling it.
There is no point in pondering why this number came up or why it appears consecutively.
What you do does not change.
Roll that dice again.
When you roll it a lot, the edge of the dice will appear.
Changing the dice frequently will not let the probability work

and you cannot extract the edge.
When you understand that it doesn't matter what comes up, you just keep rolling, there will be no more stimulation.
That is the understanding of the trader's job, the understanding of your scope of responsibility, the understanding of focusing on the process rather than the result, and its "embodiment."

When these four deep understandings are embodied as actions, it becomes no different from continuously rolling a dice, and I think this is the most succinct way to describe a true trader.
However, if there is any doubt or if you cannot keep rolling the dice, it means that the four understandings are not deep enough yet.

Many traders feel that preparing a weighted dice is difficult, but the real difficulty is "keeping rolling it."
Conversely, the reason they find it difficult to find a weighted dice is because they "cannot keep rolling it."

With that in mind, I will introduce some exercises and routines that will help you embody the understanding needed to keep rolling the dice.

- Create a stamp card
- Play with simulation software
- Create procedures
- Write
- Do not look at the account balance for a month
- Cut off social media and videos
- Keep backtesting

You might think these are very simple when you read this, but please do not underestimate them and try all of them. They are very effective.

CREATE A STAMP CARD

This exercise uses the mechanism of a stamp card given at a store.
Let's say there's a service where you get a stamp on your card each time you shop, and once you collect 20 stamps, you get a prize.
In this case, the number of attempts, 20, becomes valuable, rather than the content of what we bought.
We apply this to trading.
Here's how to do it.

First, create a stamp card with 20 spaces.
Each time you trade, check or stamp one space.
That's all you need to do.
Don't worry about winning or losing.
You just need to follow your rules and stamp one space when you do.
If you don't follow the rules, don't stamp the card.
In that case, start again from the beginning.

When you trade according to your rules, stamp one space, and when you collect 20 stamps, it means you have executed 20 rule-based trades.
Count 20 trades as one attempt.

Your goal is to collect five stamp cards with 20 stamps each.

This simple exercise is the most straightforward way to realistically feel that you are accumulating attempts.

In our experience, 20 attempts feel very long.
Many people judge based on their feelings, thinking, “I’ve done enough, but it’s not increasing,” and they prematurely judge results with an insufficient sample size, failing to maintain consistency, and abandoning the system.
In the world of probability, 20 attempts are too few.
So, count 20 trades as "one," and repeat this many times.

Making it visible with a stamp card helps you realize that you haven’t accumulated as many attempts as you think, and it helps you feel that you are steadily accumulating attempts.

When I was doing it, I wrote on the stamp card, "No matter what, complete all stamps" and "Results don’t matter."
It is effective, so please give it a try.

PLAY WITH SIMULATION SOFTWARE

This is simple but surprisingly effective in understanding the slow workings of probability and realizing that even after a losing streak, the edge will eventually prevail.
There are various services online that allow you to perform probability simulations, so look for them.
I played with Monte Carlo simulations many times, and I found it strangely calming.
To get our minds to think in probabilities, it is effective to see and experience the process and the inner workings of probability.
However, the workings of probability are slower than we think, and it is very difficult to observe the process and details in real-time.
Therefore, it is effective to use simulation software, tweak the variables, and play around with it multiple times.

You will repeatedly "experience" that no matter how badly the random distribution is skewed, it will eventually converge to the true probability.
Just knowing this as knowledge is not enough; actually

inputting variables into the simulation software and pressing buttons experimentally has a similar effect as experience.
There might be moments of slight surprise, but being surprised means that the experience has broken through your previously unconscious thoughts.
By experiencing it with surprise, like "Wow! Even with this, the probability eventually works out and I win!", your skeptical thoughts about probability will start to change.
Your thoughts will truly change when you "actually experience it."
There is nothing more convincingly persuasive than experience.
Simulation might seem like a simple exercise, but it does a wonderful job of transforming your erroneous thoughts about probability through experience.

CREATE PROCEDURES

Procedures are things other than trading rules.

I am Japanese, and in Japanese funerals, there are many procedures and customs.
These numerous procedures and customs are intentionally performed to prevent the bereaved family from being overwhelmed by deep sorrow, allowing them to pay respect to the deceased and smoothly proceed with the ceremony, which is the wisdom of our ancestors.

In trading, it's common to be overwhelmed by emotions, which can lead to chaotic actions.
By deliberately setting many procedures and customs, you can suppress actions influenced by emotions and perform the correct procedures.

For example, one procedure I often used was taking a screenshot immediately after making an entry and writing down whether all the rules that justified the entry were met.
By doing this, regardless of the subsequent market movement, I could believe that "I made the trade according to the appropriate rules," making it less likely for my emotions to be disturbed.
After settling the trade, I would take another screenshot and

again write down whether all the rules were met.
Even if the trades were losing ones, this helped me feel that I had made the necessary trades.

Additionally, collecting these screenshots gave me a sense of gathering the necessary samples, reminding me that I was trading based on probabilistic thinking.
This practice of recording immediately before and after a trade was also introduced in the way of writing a trading journal.
After a trade, take a screenshot, stamp the stamp card introduced earlier once, and close the chart.
Establish these as routines that you always follow.

You can also create routines unrelated to trading (e.g., stretching after closing the chart, making coffee, playing a musical instrument, etc.).
These routines help you focus on something else immediately after closing the chart, reducing the risk of unnecessary impulses and helping you develop habits that embody probabilistic thinking.

No matter what emotions you experience or what you think, always stick to the predetermined routines.
What you need to do is follow the process, which is already decided, and proceed according to the procedures.
That's all you need to do.

WRITE

Develop a habit of writing down your thoughts on trading and the actions you have taken.
Writing requires clarity.
Feelings and emotions are abstract, but to write them down, you must put them into words and express them in the most fitting way for yourself.
Through the process of writing, our vague feelings take shape. This not only helps you understand yourself better but also clarifies problems and identifies which processes need improvement.
The process of clarifying itself can sometimes lead to solving the problem.

When we are troubled, we are at a standstill or stagnant.
We stop because we cannot control something.
It may truly be uncontrollable, or it might just be that we believe it is, or we might be viewing it from the wrong perspective.

Talking or writing about our troubles can sometimes resolve them even if the cause of the trouble remains because we understand the scope of our control and can regain control over ourselves.

A long time ago, an acquaintance of mine, overwhelmed with debt, spoke of wanting to commit suicide.

I suggested he consult a bank, and though he thought it was hopeless, he decided to go.
When we met next, he was overjoyed because he had managed to secure a loan and could now repay his debt in manageable monthly installments.
The key point here is that the debt, the cause of his trouble, had not disappeared.
Even though the cause remained, the moment it became something within his control, the stagnation disappeared, and his troubles were resolved.

In trading, many people are unclear about what they can control and worry about things they cannot control.
What is uncontrollable creates stagnation and worry.
Unable to move forward, they continue to suffer.
By writing, we clarify everything surrounding us, identify the problems, and determine what we can do, which helps us feel more positive.

The issues we face in trading can vary from beliefs, thought processes, understanding the trader's job, trading rules, and actions, among others.
Clarifying and categorizing these into controllable and uncontrollable aspects simplifies things significantly.
The act of categorizing with words is writing.
Try writing your trading journal with this awareness.

Here are two examples of formats:

- What are you worried about?
- What do you want to do?
- What are the problems?
- What can you control?
- What is out of your control and unnecessary to think about

now?
- What can you do now?

Write what you can do and must do on sticky notes, put them where you can see them, and consider the problem resolved.

- Final goal
- List what you need to achieve it
- What can you influence?
- In what order should you proceed?
- Break it down into concrete actions
- Divide into daily tasks and make a schedule

Complete daily tasks in order

COLUMN

Concerns are Stagnation

People who are concerned are too focused on their minds.
Focusing on the mind only increases stress.
Concerns mean stagnation.
If you keep saying things like "It's painful" and "It's tough," you will only stagnate more.

It is better to focus on changing your thinking and perspective, thinking about what you can do, and creating and following steps to take action one by one.
Where are the problems in your trading?
Is it in the system, or in the consistency?
Just identifying that will help you know the next action to focus on.
Are you losing because you can't keep following the rules, or are you losing because you follow the rules but still can't win?
Clarify this and create the necessary steps to avoid stagnation.

Let me be more clear.
All mental issues are about procedures.
They are related to your beliefs and thought processes.

It's just that you haven't clarified them, but your thought processes and beliefs are automated thought procedures.
The system's rules are more practical action procedures.
Which procedure has the problem?
Everything is a procedure, and you need to clarify which procedure has the problem.
By deliberately viewing everything as a procedure, you can turn it into an actionable issue.
It's better to move something forward than to focus too much on the mind.
If you don't stagnate, it will no longer be a concern.

I understand that mental issues are not simple, but if this helps traders take a step forward from stagnation by deliberately simplifying and clarifying, it would be fortunate.

DO NOT CHECK YOUR ACCOUNT BALANCE FOR ONE MONTH

Decide not to check your account balance for one month.
If you can hide the account balance, do so; if not, make sure not to look at the area where it is displayed.

Start with one month, but as you continue, you will eventually stop checking even for three months.
I actually did this, and at first, a month felt long, and I wanted to check my account balance early. However, as I repeated it, I started finding it tedious to check and even forgot about it, eventually going three months, six months, without checking my account balance at all.

You can trade without checking your account balance, and in fact, not checking it has the advantage of reducing the risk of unnecessary anxiety and the urge to recover losses.
When calculating position sizes, some people might inadvertently look at their account balance.
This can be resolved by using a tool that automatically

calculates position sizes.

Here, as an exercise, we set a period of "one month," but the ultimate goal is to reach a state where you don't need to check it at all.
Checking once a year is sufficient.
If your funds haven't increased by then, you can think about countermeasures at that time.
If you keep changing your approach out of anxiety within a year, you won't be able to leverage the law of probability.
The problem is using a system that is so unreliable that you feel pressured within that period. Once you have created a system through thorough backtesting, commit to not changing anything for a year.
You must also acquire a long-term perspective.
If you get anxious within a month, you won't be able to achieve a long-term perspective necessary for trading calmly for a year.
Think of it as practice and try hard not to check for one month.

Checking your account balance midway has only disadvantages.
Reassuring yourself by seeing an increase is not good, nor is feeling anxious if it hasn't increased, or giving up if you see a decrease.
The more you reassure yourself by seeing an increase, the stronger the fear of losing it.
Reactions based on these values come with both sides; whether reassured or anxious, such emotional reactions increase the risk of losing consistency.

Probability doesn't emphasize individual results.

You need to perform the same action a large number of times without being swayed by interim results.
As someone trying to utilize probability, you don't need to check your account balance.
Your job is to continue doing the same thing, without changing your actions based on the account balance.
Understand this well and take on this exercise.

CUTTING OFF SNS AND VIDEOS

When you are in the stage of establishing your own method and trying to stick to it, information, trade results, and opinions from others can be a significant risk.
As someone who uses social media myself, it might seem strange for me to tell you to cut off social media, but it's more about not looking at "specific accounts or posts."

You probably look at posts where other traders explain their trading methods, views on trading, or watch videos explaining strategies, thinking they are "useful."
These can be helpful until you solidify your own method, but once you establish your own way, this information becomes a risk to your consistency.
You are the only one who understands your system the best.
Don't change your method midway just because someone else seems to be making more money.
Don't get anxious because of their opinions.
Don't feel the urge to try what they are saying immediately or to improve your system.
There is no end to it.
YouTubers will continue to provide "great strategies" forever because they need to keep posting videos.
You need to achieve consistency.

Eliminate anything that poses a risk to your consistency.

Many of you may be connected to traders who trade similarly to you, but I think it's better not to look at posts where they share their profitable trades.
You might feel like "I missed out" or think "I should have done that after all."
Other people don't matter.
Especially, the trade results or the amount of money others have made are irrelevant to you.
Being emotionally swayed by unrelated matters and having it affect your trades is a significant risk.

At least during the period when you are trying to achieve consistency, eliminate such information for your sake.
Once you achieve consistency, you won't be swayed by such information anymore.
You are currently in a very fragile state.
Consistency can easily be blown away.
Try to stay away from things that stimulate you as much as possible.

I myself completely cut off information about others' trades during certain periods when I was working on my own trades.
What you need to believe in is the system you have built and trusted through thorough backtesting.

KEEP DOING BACKTESTING

You have done backtesting with the purpose of creating a system with an edge, collecting data, and practicing, but here, you will do backtesting to engrain trading as a simple task into your body.
When you are not trading live, keep doing backtesting continuously.
Whether you win or lose doesn't matter; just keep doing backtesting as a repetitive task.
Most people lose focus and get bored, stopping halfway, but you must keep repeating it without stopping.
As you continue to do this endlessly, trading will start to feel like a truly simple task.

Wait, click, get the result, and move on to the next.
Wait, click, get the result, and move on to the next.
This cycle continues endlessly.

While doing this, you will also engage in actual trading from time to time, but it will become easier to click on trades according to the rules without thinking, just like in backtesting.

This serves as practice to engrain rule-based trading into your body and trains your eye to recognize rule-based trades from

the charts.
Most importantly, it allows you to experience firsthand how slow the effects of probability are.
Probability works very slowly, and each of your trades is so simple that it's not worth thinking about.
You will train your body to understand that trading is a series of simple tasks where thinking becomes unnecessary, and you just repeat what your body has learned.

BECOMING A MASTER OF REPETITION

- Make a stamp card
- Play with simulation software
- Create procedures
- Write
- Do not check your account balance for one month
- Cut off social media and videos
- Keep doing backtesting

If you do all the exercises introduced, you will become a master of repetition.
Most of the emotional issues you felt in trading will probably no longer appear.

To make a profit in this uncertain world of trading, you need to use the law of probability, which makes the number of trials very important.
The factor that hinders the number of trials is "yourself."
Moreover, your enthusiasm and good intentions compromise consistency.
You mistakenly believe you are constantly improving and getting better, but you are compromising consistency.

This is because you place value on wins and losses in the short term and make decisions based on short-term trials, thus being affected by randomness.
There is no end to these improvements.
At some point, you need to completely accept losing streaks and drawdowns and stop thinking about improving.

My suggestion is not to solve this with emotional control but to achieve it through complete understanding and embodiment.
1. Understand the true nature of a trader's job.
2. Verify and master the reproducibility of your edge through thorough backtesting and practice.
3. Understand probabilistic thinking and embody it through actions.
4. Understand how probability works.

You need to understand these perfectly and be able to keep repeating without bearing the responsibility for the results.
The exercises introduced will only make sense if these four understandings are deep.
If the four understandings are shallow, go back to the chapters explaining them and read them repeatedly.
Write these ideas in your trading journal in your own words, and be able to explain them to someone else.

Ultimately, you need to train not just to understand them in your head, but to make them natural actions.
Once you understand the four points well, do all the exercises I introduced properly.
This way, you will be able to keep repeating actions based on probabilistic trials "without thinking."

EMOTIONAL ISSUES

While we recognize the importance of consistency, achieving it feels very difficult.
Many people think they can't win because of their emotions.
Emotions are not the cause; they are the result.
Emotions reflect the results of your incorrect thought processes and beliefs.

If you view emotions as the cause, the only things you can do are mastering breathing techniques or practicing Zen, as often suggested.
However, if you view emotions as the result, you can focus on the underlying causes and achieve deeper problem-solving.
If you experience emotional highs and lows in trading or find it difficult to stick to your rules due to intense emotions, it is because of your incorrect thought processes and beliefs that place value on wins and losses, leading to those emotions as a result.

What matters are your understanding of the market, the job of a trader and its scope of responsibility, your system, and how probability works.
A deep understanding of these aspects will enable you to approach your work regardless of the results.
When these deep understandings are integrated into one and embodied in your actions, the emotional issues experienced

by many traders will no longer appear.

I don't do emotional control at all.
However, I am not an emotionless person and am quite emotional in daily life.
Regarding trading, I genuinely don't care about the immediate results, so no emotions arise that need to be dealt with.
This is because I have trained myself over a long period.
I have focused on deepening the necessary understandings and embodying them through my actions.
I have eliminated all habits that I shouldn't have and trained myself not to contradict the beliefs I want to adopt.
This is because I consider emotions to be the result, not the cause.

This is also clearly written in "Trading in the Zone" by Mark Douglas, a very famous book in the trading world.
"Trading in the Zone" is considered the bible of trading psychology and is read by many people worldwide.
Despite this, many people still advocate for "emotional control."
Mark Douglas repeatedly states in "Trading in the Zone" that excellent traders don't perceive market information as painful or recognize it as containing negative information.
He also clearly states that beliefs create this pain.
The difference between top traders and others is that they "don't fear"; nothing else sets them apart.

This guided my path.
My system is a simple trend-following system using Dow Theory and multiple time frames.
It consists only of the basics found in any textbook, but I have

deepened my understanding to a practical level.
Regarding trading psychology, I have simply deepened my understanding of "Trading in the Zone."
In other words, I don't do anything special beyond the basics.
The key is how deeply you can understand the basics.
Although many people have read "Trading in the Zone," they haven't deepened their understanding and have misunderstood the content.
While writing this article, I revisited various online explanations of "Trading in the Zone" and found that most people missed the most crucial part: that solving emotional issues lies in beliefs.
Some even forced their reasoning that "emotional control is essential" and tied it to probabilistic thinking, which fundamentally don't connect.

Please revisit "Trading in the Zone" with this perspective.
You will likely discover something new.
And if you haven't read it yet, please do so when you have the chance.

COLUMN

"Don't Watch the Pot" Theory

Our job as traders is to prepare a system with an edge and consistently repeat it, accumulating trade samples to leverage probabilities and extract the edge.
Utilizing probabilities takes time, and the issue we face is maintaining consistency.

Understanding the sample size required for probabilities to work and the time needed to gather them, along with trusting the system's edge and recognizing that individual outcomes are irrelevant, addresses the consistency issue.

Problems arise when you focus on results within a timeframe where probabilities haven't had a chance to work.
You must focus on the process and ignore short-term results, but this becomes difficult if you pay attention to immediate outcomes.
Therefore, it's important to clarify your necessary processes and eliminate anything else from your actions.

I call this the "Don't Watch the Pot" Theory.
It's like when boiling water; if you watch the pot, it seems to

take forever, but if you do something else, you find the water boiling when you check back.
Many traders struggle to extract their edge because they keep watching the pot.

Reduce the need to watch your charts as much as possible in your trading.
For example, in day trading, price movements take time, so you shouldn't need to watch the chart constantly after entering a trade.
Set appropriate stop losses, calculate when you need to check again, set alarms, or set price alerts and walk away from the chart.
Additionally, monitoring the P&L during a trade is unnecessary for your process.
You need to hide it or avoid looking at it.
Avoid anything not related to your process.
Focusing on the process is crucial, but conversely, anything outside the process is dangerous.
The rule is to stay away from dangerous things as much as possible.

The problem in trading stems from the short-sightedness that undermines your consistency.
You are focusing on the wrong place.
Don't watch the pot.
You don't need to watch the pot until the water boils.
Do something else.
It may sound simple, but it is very important.

SUMMARY

Let's summarize what you need to do to succeed in trading.

Create a strategy and backtest it with a large sample size.
Always trade based on fixed entry and exit rules.
If you can confirm that your capital gradually increases, implement the strategy in real trading (or forward testing).

Strictly adhere to the rules of what not to do.
Do not look at charts unnecessarily, do not check your profits and losses, and do not check your account balance.
In real trading, the only thing that matters is how you can maintain consistency and keep repeating the same actions.
Avoid habits and actions that focus on the results.

In short, this is all you need to do.
If you think about or do anything extra, you will not succeed because you cannot maintain consistency and the probability will not work in your favor.

Be prepared to repeat the pre-tested trades no matter what, even if your capital decreases over the year.
Stop trying to make improvements.
No matter what happens, continue to repeat the same trades.
I understand your concern about the future, but the future is never guaranteed, so you must make up your mind at some point.

No matter the losing streaks or drawdowns, be determined to repeat the same trades for one year.
If you adhere to the capital management based on the performance of the pre-tested system, things won't go too wrong.
Whether the probability works or not will be known in a year anyway.
Make sure you don't change anything midway within the year.
Once you decide to commit for a year and start working on it, you will take your first step as a trader.

The skill of a trader is consistency, not how much money you make.
Once you decide to repeat the same trades no matter what, you will start growing as a trader.
Do not worry about the results.
The results reflect the system's performance, not your performance as a trader.
Aim to be an excellent trader.
Aim to be a trader who can continue to do the same thing calmly, no matter how many losses you encounter.

CHAPTER 2: CREATING THE MINDSET OF AN EXCELLENT TRADER

No matter how excellent the system is, if the person using it does not have the optimal mindset of a trader, the system's edge cannot be fully realized.

To transform you into a true trader, I will introduce the necessary mindset and ways of thinking.

Although I write about various topics, they are all deeply connected as a single concept, and I repeatedly convey the same ideas.

You can start reading from any section that interests you, so read a section daily.

Read these repeatedly and rewrite your mindset into that of a trader.

COMPLETELY CHANGE YOUR PERCEPTION OF RESULTS

As I have repeatedly mentioned, to succeed in trading, you need to abandon responsibility for the results.
You are not responsible for the results.
Your job is only to keep following the rules.

Additionally, let's completely change the way we judge results as "good" or "bad."
I don't like using the terms "win" and "lose" as they are unconsciously tied to "good" and "bad" judgments, but whether you win or lose, neither is good or bad.
It is neither success nor failure.
Understand this completely.

A successful trade is one that follows the rules.
A failed trade is one that does not follow the rules.

The results of wins and losses continue to appear before us, influenced by randomness.
There is no need to cling to them, nor is there any point in

labeling them as success or failure.

To completely change your perception of results, deeply understand probabilistic thinking.
The more you understand that you are utilizing probability, the more your perception of each result as "good" or "bad" will change.

PROBABILISTIC THINKING

The world of trading is a world of uncertainty.
Short-term results are random; you can lose even if you enter a trade correctly, and you can win even if you enter haphazardly.
In this world governed by randomness, it is essential to think in terms of probability.
Even if short-term results are random, repeating the same trade many times will reveal the probabilistic edge of that trade.

This is similar to coin tossing.
If you toss a coin five times, you might get heads all five times.
Looking only at this part, the probability of heads appears to be 100%.
However, if you continue tossing the coin 1000 times or 10,000 times, it will converge to the true probability of 50%.
This is the law of large numbers.
To make probability work in trading, you need to trade under the same conditions.
This is why discipline and consistency are said to be important.

We must thoroughly investigate what happens when we

repeat a trade and then replicate that trade in actual trading.
What is required of traders is consistency, and probability works over the large sample size collected over time.
If you understand this, you will naturally understand what not to do.
What you should not do is break the rules, prioritize short-term wins and losses, and contaminate the sample you collect with impurities.
By acquiring probabilistic thinking, you will naturally understand what you should really do, what you should not do, and develop the thought process of a trader.

What we need is sample size.
Sample size is also important in backtesting.
As explained with the coin toss example, the reliability of statistical edge increases with sample size.
The larger the trade sample, the more reliable the system's edge.
Since we cannot know the future and must always trade in a state of uncertainty about the outcome, we need to use systems that have been tested with large sample sizes and continue to collect large sample sizes in actual trading over time.

DRAWING OUT THE EDGE OF THE SYSTEM

Once you have conducted backtesting with a large sample size and confirmed that the system has an edge, you need to draw it out in actual trading.
To do this, you must repeat the trades in the same way as the backtesting.

"Drawing out the edge of the system" does not involve doing anything special.
It simply means maintaining consistency.
The key is how thoroughly you have tested in advance and how well you have been able to define the rules down to the smallest details.
You aim to conduct consistent trades to draw out the system's edge in real trading.
However, you will encounter various problems that hinder consistency.
Fear of entry, anxiety while holding positions, anger and disappointment after a stop loss, and the temptation to tweak or change the system after a losing streak—all of these things will try to disrupt your consistency.

This is a test of consistency.
You must pass this test and prove through your actions that you have the necessary mindset as a trader.
This is the path of trials for a trader.

Many traders believe that having a system or strategy with an edge will immediately lead to profits.
However, this is not the case.
It takes time to draw out the edge from those strategies and systems.
Many traders lack the qualities and consistency required as traders, and even if they have a system or strategy with an edge, they cannot draw out that edge.

You must grow as a trader.
You need to understand the true job of a trader, the scope of its responsibilities, focus only on what you should do, and let go of what you cannot control.
When your mindset and actions fully align with those of a trader, drawing out the edge from the system becomes easy.

USING AN UNTESTED SYSTEM IS GAMBLING AND INHERENTLY RISKY

If you are trading with probabilistic thinking, you must conduct backtesting.
Using an untested system is absolutely unacceptable.
You must never do it.
This is because without understanding the system, you have no information necessary for trading.

You need to know in advance whether the system has an edge by testing it with a large sample size.
By large, I mean at least 1000 times.
You cannot test this number in real trading.
It takes too much time, and it is nearly impossible to continue 1000 trades without knowing if it's right or wrong.
And if it turns out to be wrong, you'll have to start another 1000 trades with a different approach.
This is highly inefficient.
It is very difficult to create a system with an edge by doing only a few sets of these 1000 trades.

By backtesting with a sample size of over 1000, you can get a reasonably accurate idea of the system's performance.
This allows you to determine an appropriate position size that can be safely managed in the long term with a 0% risk of ruin based on the system's performance.
With a small number of trials, such as 100, you can roughly tell if there is an edge, but it is not accurate because it is heavily influenced by randomness.

Moreover, backtesting also serves as practice.
Even if a system has an edge, being able to accurately identify signals from actual charts and continuously enter trades correctly is another matter and requires practice.
Just as in any field, a few hundred practices are not enough to become a professional; trading requires thorough practice as well.

Consistency is crucial when trading with probabilistic thinking.
Without consistency, it is impossible to collect a large number of trade samples under the same conditions.
However, trying to maintain consistency in real trading brings various challenges.
This is where your understanding of probability and trust in the system are tested.
Trusting probability and the system means trusting the statistics.
This reliability is built by a large sample size.
A few results are influenced by randomness and cannot be trusted, but those tested with a massive sample size reflect probabilities more accurately.
This is because the law of large numbers is at work.

To maintain consistency in real trading and actually draw out the system's edge, you need to conduct thorough backtesting in advance.
It may seem tedious, but it is one of the important jobs of a trader and a necessary preparation.

THE LAW OF LARGE NUMBERS AND HOW PROBABILITY WORKS

When utilizing probability, it is essential to understand how probability works.

The larger the sample size, the more accurately it reflects the true probability.

For example, if you flip a coin only five times, you might get heads every time.

With five heads out of five flips, the probability appears to be 100%.

However, this small number of trials is influenced by randomness and does not reflect the true probability.

As you continue flipping the coin, increasing the trials to 100, 1000, and 10000, the results will converge to the true probability.

This is called the law of large numbers.

To make the law of large numbers work, you need to accumulate many trials, which takes time.

During this time, the results will be influenced by randomness, so traders must understand that probability works slower than they might expect.

In trading, it is not just a matter of winning percentage but also incorporating favorable risk-reward ratios.
Therefore, you can increase your capital even before the probabilities fully converge.
Even if randomness affects the results to some extent, your capital can grow.
As you continue repeating these trades, the overall performance will eventually converge to the true probability.
This means that even though the annual performance may vary due to randomness, it will ultimately reflect the system's true performance.

By understanding the accurate performance of your system through extensive backtesting with a large sample size, you can determine whether a particular year's performance is an outlier due to randomness.
This prevents you from becoming overly confident or anxious.

To make probability work, you need to collect a large number of trade samples under the same conditions.
This is why traders need discipline, consistency, and patience.
Traders are constantly tested for their consistency.
The beliefs, thought processes, and corresponding emotions such as greed and fear can disrupt consistency.
The market constantly tests your consistency through losing streaks, drawdowns, and the presence or intensity of emotions like greed and fear.
The market tests whether you have the right beliefs, thought processes, and habits to be a profitable trader.

Maintaining this consistency requires a thorough understanding of how probability works.

NOT VALUING WINS AND LOSSES

We all start trading with the intention to make money, so from the beginning, we have the belief that "winning is good, losing is bad."
This means that we start trading in a state where succeeding in trading is very difficult.
Because the world of trading is a world of uncertainty.

To gain certainty in a world of uncertainty, we need to use the law of probability.
To make probability work, consistency is important, and we need to gather a large number of trading samples under the same conditions.
At this time, if you have the belief that wins and losses have value, you will be swayed by short-term randomness and won't be able to maintain consistency.

When you are influenced by randomness, even the most strategic edge will lose, and even the most random entries will win.
Your losses might just be random.
Facing this randomness with the belief that "winning is good, losing is bad" leads you into an endless loop of improvements without answers.

Even if there is no reason, you will immediately tweak the system, failing to trade consistently and unable to utilize the edge of the system through probability.

What's important is not to value wins and losses.
This is easy to say but very difficult to actually do.
First, start by understanding it in your head, and eventually, you need to reflect it in your actions.

Without valuing wins and losses, you must deeply understand how to win.
By deeply understanding probabilistic thinking, you can shift from valuing wins and losses to valuing the "number of properly executed samples."
This is the perspective of a casino owner.
The casino owner doesn't care about who is winning how much today.
They know that with enough samples, the casino will eventually win.

CONSISTENCY

What is required of a true trader is consistency.
It is no exaggeration to say that this is everything.
A trader's job is not to win or lose the trade in front of them, but to consistently operate a system with a confirmed statistical edge without wavering, and to leverage the law of probability to draw out the system's edge.

For a true trader, any problem that occurs in real trading is a problem of consistency.
It is not a problem of strategy or system.
This is because they already have strategies and systems tested with large sample sizes.
Many traders trade to achieve immediate wins without testing their strategies or systems, which leads them to fight the random price movements of the market, constantly being trapped in an endless loop of adjustments to match randomness.
They continuously change their strategies, mistakenly believing they are making progress, but in reality, they are being swayed by randomness and going nowhere.

True traders who trade with probabilistic thinking use systems tested with large sample sizes that transcend randomness, so they are not swayed by the immediate results.
The important thing is how to maintain consistency, and that

becomes the battle.
To be more specific, the challenge is to ensure that your confidence in your statistics is not shaken by randomness.

This challenge relates to how many incorrect beliefs you have left, how well you understand probabilistic thinking, how well you understand what you are doing, how much you trust your statistics, whether you have tested with a reliable sample size, and how much you have eliminated bad habits.
This is the challenge for us traders who trade with probabilistic thinking.

The market will try to shake your confidence in your system and break your consistency through losing streaks, drawdowns, and various other events.
In reality, the market is not doing anything to you, but your trader's thought processes and beliefs react to these events, creating pain and distrust.
This is why I often say, "You are constantly being tested for consistency."

You need to look at yourself, always note down the problems that arise, consider the causes, and if necessary, create rules regarding your actions and deal with them.

THE THOUGHT PROCESSES BEHIND EMOTIONS ARE IMPORTANT

In trading, emotions can hinder consistent actions and lead to disastrous behavior.
Many people do not realize that it is not the emotions themselves that are bad, but the thought processes and beliefs behind those emotions that are the root of the problem.
If the thought processes or beliefs that trigger those emotions are eliminated, the emotions that interfere with trading will no longer arise.
However, this does not mean that all emotions in everyday life will disappear from that person.

Every trader starts trading with the desire to make money, so they initially have the mistaken belief of "valuing wins and losses."
If this belief changes, the reason to fear losing will disappear, and the actions to avoid it will also disappear.
This does not mean that the person has become emotionless.
It simply means that there is no longer a reason to feel fear

regarding this matter.

When people talk about eliminating emotions, many imagine an emotionless person in everyday life and misunderstand, but it is not that.
It means "not generating bad emotions related to trading."
To achieve this, we replace the incorrect thought processes and beliefs related to trading with correct ones.

PROPER UNDERSTANDING OF TRADING SOLVES THE ROOT OF THE PROBLEM

Emotions are generated by thought processes and beliefs.
To address emotional issues, we need to drain energy from incorrect thought processes and beliefs and infuse energy into new beliefs.
This topic was mentioned in Mark Douglas's book and is extremely important for becoming a trader without fear and solving the root of the problem.
If you truly believe that "the win or loss of the trade in front of you does not determine success," you will no longer have reasons to be intensely angry or fearful because of losses.

For example, when I was a child, I was very afraid of riding roller coasters, but after riding them many times, I came to believe, "I won't die from this."
Even though I still felt a little fear, this understanding was reinforced by experience each time I rode.

The energy of the old belief, "roller coasters are dangerous," was discharged, and the belief, "roller coasters are safe," accumulated energy, and now I feel no fear at all.
People who are afraid of roller coasters might look at me and think I am very mentally strong, but it is not because I have strong willpower or am good at controlling my emotions.
I just have different beliefs, and there is no reason for me to feel fear.
If this example does not resonate, consider the difference between people who are afraid of flying and those who are not.
People who are not afraid of flying are not better at controlling their emotions or more emotionless than those who are afraid.
They simply have different thought processes and beliefs.

The same can be said for trading.
Many people try to cope with emotional control alone while holding incorrect beliefs, but this is the wrong approach.
It is important to create a situation where there is no reason to feel fear.
To do this, it is crucial to understand correctly that short-term wins and losses do not determine success and to actually gain that experience.
This is the fundamental solution and the truth about emotional issues that many people are not even aware of.

IT'S IMPORTANT NOT TO RECOGNIZE LOSSES AS BAD

When you have a system with an edge and you are trying to draw out that edge in real trading, consistency becomes the problem.
As long as you maintain consistency, the law of large numbers will work, and you will be able to draw out the edge.
Conversely, if you cannot maintain consistency, the system will fail.

I explained that a proper understanding of trading solves the root of the problem, and one of those proper understandings is "not recognizing losses as bad."
We recognize losses as bad things, things to avoid, things to learn from, and every time we encounter a loss, we generate negative emotions from them.
This is what causes the loss of consistency.
If you perceive losses as bad, things to avoid, or things to learn from, you will always fall into the trap of constant improvement or system adjustments and will not be able to escape the loop of randomness.

The edge of the system includes losses.

What is important is that all the losses that occur when repeating the system are included, and in the end, there is a positive result.
For this, you must not recognize losses as bad and must not generate negative emotions from them.
What you should avoid is tampering with a system that has an edge, and you must absolutely stay on that path.

By following the rules no matter what happens and continuing to do so for a long time, the law of large numbers will work, probabilities will converge, and the edge of the system will be drawn out.
This is why discipline, consistency, and patience are said to be important in trading.

To actually embody discipline, consistency, and patience, you need to make decisions based on discipline, not on wins or losses.
You should judge the success or failure of a trade not by whether you won or lost but by whether you followed the discipline or broke it.
When you stop recognizing losses as bad and replace judgments based on wins and losses with judgments based on discipline, trading becomes very simple.

RESULTS ARE RANDOM

Short-term results are random.
No matter how perfectly you execute a trade with an edge, you can still lose, and no matter how randomly you enter a trade, you can still win.
However, if you repeat the trades over a long period, the inherent probabilities emerge from the randomness.
It is crucial to understand that the world of the market is a world of uncertainty, and short-term results are random.

That losing streak might be random, and that drawdown might be random.
Individual results are not related to each other, and whether you lost the last trade has no bearing on the next result.
Losing the last trade is not a reason to fear the next trade, and a losing streak does not negate the edge of your system.

You must not make inferences based on randomness.
There is no answer there, and it will always make you feel like you have finally figured it out, only to shatter that feeling in the next moment, trapping you in a loop that ultimately leads to despair.

You need to understand that short-term results are random and understand what kind of thinking and behavior are necessary to profit in this uncertain world.

Probability is random in the short term but converges to its true probability in the long term.
To harness the law of probability, the key is to ignore short-term randomness and consistently repeat the same actions over the long term.
The way to achieve consistent profits from this uncertain market is to use a system whose edge has been proven through backtesting over a large sample size over a long period and to consistently and disciplinedly follow the system's instructions.

DON'T REGRET LOSSES, REGRET NOT FOLLOWING THE RULES

It's often said that you should learn from losses, but once you've created a system with an edge, you don't need to learn from losses.
Those who need to learn from losses are those who are in the process of creating a system with an edge.

If you try to learn from every loss, you will unconsciously seek a 100% win rate and recognize losses as something to avoid.
This perception is the furthest from success in trading, which is influenced by randomness.
This is because it is impossible to avoid losses.
Attempting the impossible results in a 0% success rate.

Short-term results are random, and no matter how perfectly you enter a trade, you can still lose.
Even if you seek meaning in the random results that occur, there is nothing there.

Because it is random.
You have conducted backtests through large sample sizes in advance and know how probabilities converge when you repeat those trades.
So, what is there to reflect on about the results of trades that followed the rules?
What you need to reflect on is when you didn't follow the rules.

When you don't follow the rules, even if it was a winning trade, you need to reflect seriously.
At that point, you have deviated from the system and abandoned the system with an edge.
You might have won that trade by chance, but winning isn't everything.
If you break the rules and win, it becomes a wrong success experience, and you will easily break the rules next time.
Every time you are about to lose, you will think, "just this time," and break the rules, but gradually you won't even think about it, and breaking the rules will become the norm.
You can't keep avoiding losses forever, and until you face a disastrous outcome, that bad habit will continue.

The losses that occur by following the rules are not bad or something to avoid.
They are what ultimately form the edge of the system.
Since they are not bad, there is no need to reflect on them.
If you followed the rules, you did nothing wrong.
Please understand this well.

STOP LOSSES ARE PROOF THAT THE SYSTEM IS WORKING

Many people think that when a stop loss occurs, the system is not functioning or that the system's edge is not being drawn out, but this is incorrect.
A stop loss that occurs by following the rules is proof that the system is functioning, and there is an edge in that stop loss.
By adhering to the rules and executing the stop loss at that point, you will ultimately be left with a profit.

The system is not designed to win single trades in front of you.
It is designed to be operated so that after experiencing all the wins and losses that occur according to its rules, you are left with a profit.
Executing a stop loss according to the system's rules unequivocally means that the system's edge is being exercised.

Many people use the system to win the trade in front of them, which creates a contradiction with probabilistic thinking.
A statistical edge means that there is an edge in the total of wins and losses, so trying to avoid only losses while trying to

draw out the statistical edge is contradictory.
You need to follow the system and execute stop losses, and if you have not deviated from the rules, consider that the edge is being exercised.
This is not merely an assumption but a fact.
It takes time for this to manifest visibly as profit, so you just haven't recognized that there is an edge in stop losses yet.

Think long-term, not in terms of single trades.
The system is designed to be profitable when operated repeatedly.
It is already assumed that stop losses will occur, so you should feel assured when executing stop losses.
From now on, consider that executing stop losses according to the rules means the system is working and the edge is being exercised.

ABANDON RESPONSIBILITY FOR WINS AND LOSSES

As long as you follow the rules of the system, the wins and losses that occur are part of the system and are not your responsibility.

To succeed in trading with probabilistic thinking, it is crucial to abandon responsibility for wins and losses.
You should not try to control what you cannot control.
Doing so only complicates the problem and makes it unsolvable.

Even the best systems will experience losing streaks and drawdowns.
During losing streaks, many people become anxious, try to improve the system, or abandon it midway, thinking it no longer works.
The biggest risk is yourself.
Your enthusiasm and desire to win become risks.
You fiddle with the system, feeling like you're doing something necessary and making progress, but you are continuously undermining consistency and can never escape the loop of constant improvement.

You must continue to do the same thing during losing streaks and drawdowns.
As long as any system experiences losing streaks and drawdowns, you must believe in it fully.
Otherwise, no matter what system you use, you will never pass the test of discipline and consistency, nor will you be able to draw out its edge.
Every system will have a test of discipline and consistency due to losing streaks and drawdowns.
This test is unavoidable, so at some point, you must believe in the system fully.
The key is whether you tested the system thoroughly enough beforehand to trust it.

As long as you follow the rules of the system, the wins and losses that occur are part of the system.
No matter how long the losing streak, it won't matter if the law of large numbers is in effect.
This is because it includes probability.
In other words, accepting losing streaks and drawdowns means you have finally accepted the system and can draw out its true edge.

If all losses, losing streaks, and drawdowns are part of forming the system's edge, you have nothing to worry about.
Your job is only to act according to the rules; everything else is not your job or your responsibility.
If you have thoroughly backtested the system and understand and trust it, believe in it until the end.
Although it feels very long to us, do not draw conclusions with only about 30 trials.

If you have prepared well, create and adapt analogies like the boss mode and employee mode I introduced previously to clearly define your job and responsibilities as a trader.

Understanding that you are not responsible for the immediate results will make it easier to focus on the process and pass the test of discipline and consistency.

ABSOLUTELY FOLLOW THE RULES

You must always follow the rules.
There is no choice between following or not following them.
You absolutely must follow them.

The fundamental reason why you cannot follow the rules is that you do not deeply understand or truly believe that following the rules leads to success.
You prioritize the immediate wins and losses, do not trade with probabilistic thinking, do not fully believe in the statistical edge of the system, or lack the understanding that there is an edge in taking losses according to the rules.
Even if you think you understand probabilistic thinking, if you truly do not, you will easily break the rules.
Breaking the rules indicates that you value the immediate trade more than probabilities or statistics.
Your actions reflect your beliefs and thought processes, so if you are breaking the rules, you do not truly understand.

Losses are not bad.
You end up with profits because you take losses according to the rules.
You must understand this statistically.
Many traders do not understand this and think, "The system

didn't work this time" when they incur a loss.
That is not the case.
The system is working.
There is an edge in losses that occur by following the rules.
Understand this well.
Breaking the rules means you have abandoned your job as a trader to draw out the system's edge.

Reflect not on the losses but on not following the rules.
Once a system with an edge is created through large sample size backtesting, the problem is no longer the system but you.
Always check if you are maintaining consistency.

If you have a clear understanding of your role as a trader over a long time frame, an understanding of probabilistic thinking and how probabilities work, and an understanding and trust in the system, you will not break the rules.

HUMAN INSTINCTIVELY AVOID UNCERTAINTY AND LOSS

We instinctively try to avoid uncertainty and loss.
We prefer what we already know and certainty over the unknown future. However, markets are random in the short term, with no certainties.
This means that trading based on instinct will almost certainly not satisfy that instinct.

How can we succeed in trading by resisting the instinct to avoid uncertainty?
The answer is "don't resist."
Uncertainty appears when we focus on immediate trading results.
By shifting our perspective and looking at a longer time frame, we can discover certainty.
When we focus on this certainty, it aligns with what our instinct seeks, allowing us to act without conflict or resistance to our instincts.

How much you can focus on certainty depends on how truly you recognize and understand it.
In other words, it's crucial to have conviction backed by probabilistic thinking and thorough backtesting experience.

Backtesting is not just about collecting data; its aspect as practice is extremely important.
Many people think they've done enough backtesting, but if emotional issues arise in real trading, you haven't done enough practice-oriented backtesting.
When you repeat backtesting to the point of exhaustion, you collect a large sample size and experience the results, leading you to lose sense of value in a single trade before you.

Those who feel anxiety or fear in real trading are still placing high value on immediate wins and losses, and this belief manifests as emotions of anxiety and fear.
You must experience the results of backtesting, not just treat them as data.
Merely knowing the data leads to anxiety, doubts arise even with a few consecutive losses, and you quickly focus on immediate uncertainty, causing distress.

Those lacking practice tend to dislike stop-losses and consecutive losses even in backtesting.
You need to repeat backtesting until you feel absolutely nothing, until it becomes completely mechanical. Backtesting allows for accumulating a far larger sample size than real trading, with time passing more quickly, making it easier to think from a broader perspective and gain experience.

If you don't become completely desensitized at the backtesting stage, you'll naturally suffer from immediate results in real trading. Make sure to conduct thorough practice-oriented backtesting.

When our perspective shifts from uncertain short-term results to long-term certainty, the instinct to avoid uncertainty stops working, allowing us to act without contradiction.
And to change our perspective from short-term to long-term through experience, backtesting, which has a faster time progression than real trading, is most efficient.
Make sure to practice thoroughly.

THE MISCONCEPTION THAT YOU CAN'T SUCCEED BECAUSE YOU CAN'T CONTROL YOUR EMOTIONS

Many traders believe that they could succeed if only they didn't have emotional issues.
They think that emotions are the cause of all their problems, but emotions are not the cause—they are the result.
Emotions that hinder your success in trading arise because you have thought processes and beliefs that hinder your success in trading.
Emotions are merely signals reflecting those thought processes and beliefs.

By the way, I don't engage in what is commonly referred to as "emotional control" at all.
This is because emotional problems don't occur in my trading

in the first place.
If they don't occur, there's no need to deal with them.
Whenever I say this, someone always says, "But you're human, so you have emotions," or "Emotions are inevitable."
But that's not what I'm talking about.
Don't misunderstand me—I'm not an emotionless person.
When it comes to trading, I have trained myself to perceive phenomena that most people find frightening or anxiety-inducing through different thought processes and perceptions, so I simply don't see them as scary.

To explain with a familiar example, I'm not afraid of flying at all.
But it's not because I'm a master of emotional control.
People who are afraid of flying wouldn't see me as a master of emotional control.
I fear frogs, but some people don't.
Are they masters of emotional control?
It's simply a difference in perception.

Regarding trading, most emotional issues stem from incorrect thought processes or beliefs.
The idea that losing is bad, that it takes you further from success, that you're unsure if the system has an edge—these thought processes lead you to label wins and losses as "good" or "bad" and react accordingly.
Their emotional problems stem from ignorance.

For example:
- Reckless position sizing: not thinking statistically based on risk of ruin, not understanding the system.
- Fear of immediate losses: shallow understanding of probabilistic thinking, not realizing the insignificance of a

single trade's impact, not verifying the system's edge.
- Joyful when winning, sad when losing: thinking that the responsibility for wins and losses lies with them, believing that wins and losses determine success, not understanding how probability works, lacking understanding that even with an edge, it may take months to see gains.

Understanding is everything.
If you understand the system's performance, the safe position size to continuously operate the system, that individual wins and losses pose no threat to you, how slowly probabilities play out, that your responsibility lies not in wins and losses but in following the rules, and that losses have an edge, you will have nothing to fear.
There would be no reason to fear the next trade.
They are not lacking emotional control but are having terrifying experiences due to a lack of understanding.
If you don't stop trading based on ignorance, you'll go bankrupt regardless of how well you control your emotions.
Saying "I'm not bothered because I can control my emotions" after going bankrupt is meaningless.

There is much to be done before concluding that emotions are the cause of everything.
Study trading thoroughly.
Develop probabilistic thinking.
Conduct thorough backtesting and practice extensively.
Gain a broader perspective and find the edge in losses.
Size your positions with a 0% risk of ruin based on system performance.

After doing all this, ask yourself again how you perceive immediate losses.

If you're still afraid, examine the thought processes or beliefs causing it.
Eliminating the reasons for fear and anxiety through understanding is the fundamental solution, making emotional control unnecessary, which is the best form of "emotional control."

HESITATION

There are several reasons why you might hesitate to enter a trade.

1. Hesitation indicates unclear trading points:
If your rules are vague, you might struggle with deciding whether to enter a trade.
If you find yourself hesitating, make your rules more precise so that you won't hesitate next time.
Although the market can sometimes be ambiguous, it's crucial to decide in advance how you will act when you are unsure.
You need to backtest to statistically determine which approach is more advantageous in such situations.

For example, I always choose to enter a trade when I find it genuinely difficult to decide.
This is because my tests have shown that the cost of missed opportunities is greater.
For me, this rule has a statistical edge.
Deciding in advance allows you to enter trades without hesitation or regret, regardless of the outcome.

2. Hesitation due to past losses:
You might hesitate because of the memory of a recent stop loss or a streak of losses, thinking, "What if I lose again?"
This requires a change in perspective.

First, understand that the previous trade and the current trade are unrelated, and a stop loss is not something to fear.
The system with an edge ensures profits by following the rules and taking stop losses.
Losses can continue due to randomness, and losing streaks are inevitable.
You have already backtested with a large sample size anticipating these scenarios.
If backtesting confirms that your system has an edge, following the rules and taking stop losses will ultimately yield profits, so there's no need to worry.
Hesitating due to past trades and not following your rules disrupts consistency, which is the real issue.

3. Hesitation due to disbelief in the system's statistical edge:
This hesitation stems from fear or anxiety due to uncertainty.
The solution is simple: conduct more backtesting.
If you don't believe in your system's statistical edge, you'll lose consistency during inevitable losing streaks and drawdowns.
Ensure that you conduct thorough backtesting with a large sample size.

I've introduced three causes and their solutions, but most issues can be resolved through proper preparation.
Preparation is vital in trading.
If you hesitate, consider it a sign that your preparation is insufficient and make the necessary preparations.

STOP LOSSES AND POSITION SIZE

It's often said, "If you can't take stop losses, reduce your position size," or "If you're scared, reduce your position size." However, the fundamental reason for not being able to take stop losses is not the position size but a lack of understanding of a trader's job.

First, your position size should not be determined by your emotions.
If you trade with an unreasonable position size because you feel "emotionally okay," you will end up bankrupt.
Your emotions are irrelevant; you must trade with a position size that ensures a 0% risk of ruin based on your system's performance.

Emotional issues arise from problems in thought processes and beliefs, such as a negative perception of stop losses, a lack of understanding of the system's performance, or a lack of trust in the system.
Therefore, even if you reduce your position size to ease your mind, your funds won't increase if you don't understand the system or if the system lacks an edge.

If you have thoroughly tested your system, understand its performance, have trust in it, and apply probabilistic thinking

to adopt a position size with a 0% risk of ruin, you will understand what you are doing and won't feel fear.
Naturally, you will no longer have trouble taking stop losses because you understand that stop losses are part of the system and that there is an edge in stop losses.

Therefore, the commonly heard advice to reduce position size if you can't take stop losses is not fundamental by itself.
Without a fundamental solution, it only extends the time until bankruptcy slightly.
This is because those who reduce their position size due to emotions, without understanding the essence, may easily increase their position size again if randomness temporarily works in their favor and they experience a winning streak.
As long as your decision-making is based on emotions, it is impossible to succeed in trading, and for these reasons, reducing position size to ease emotions only serves as a temporary measure.

Your trading problems cannot be solved merely by changing your position size.
Learn trading thoroughly, understand probabilistic thinking, conduct extensive backtesting, practice rigorously, and build an understanding and trust in your system.
This will naturally lead you to appropriate position sizing and ensure you avoid bankruptcy.

THE CONTRADICTION OF FEARING IMMEDIATE LOSSES WHILE USING A SYSTEM

If you are using a system you believe in, fearing the immediate loss is contradictory.
This indicates that you do not fully trust the system.
You become sensitive to immediate results because you haven't thoroughly tested the system and are unsure if it has an edge.
If you have thoroughly tested the system beforehand, your perspective would be long-term, and immediate results wouldn't bother you.
Without testing the system, you cannot trade based on the trust in its statistical edge.

Examine yourself before and during trading to see if you are fearful.
If you feel fear, it suggests a lack of backtesting or an inadequate understanding of probabilistic thinking.

In such cases, you need to perform thorough backtesting again.

You might think you have already gathered enough backtesting data, but backtesting is not just about data collection.
Its role as practice is extremely important.
You need to build confidence based on the experience that you can handle the system accurately.
This is not just about the technical ability to act according to the rules but about having the confidence from experience that you can trade relaxed, knowing that you will profit in the long term by repeatedly trading.
By thoroughly conducting backtesting as practice, you will build understanding and trust in the system, and trust in yourself.
By having prior experience that you can repeat trades without worrying about inevitable losing streaks and drawdowns, your trading will become easier.
This confidence in leveraging the statistical edge will eliminate the contradiction of fearing immediate losses while using a system.

DON'T PREDICT THE MARKET; YOUR OPINION IS JUST A HINDRANCE

What is crucial in trading is to consistently use a thoroughly tested system and let probability work on the gathered samples to draw out the edge.
Short-term results are random; even perfect trades can end in a stop loss, and poorly executed trades can sometimes win.
Because of this randomness, predicting the outcome of an individual trade is meaningless.
All you need to do is follow the pre-tested rules that yield profits in the long run.

The reason you trade should be simply "because it's the rule."
You don't need predictions or opinions like "it looks like it will go up."
Having these views makes you more susceptible to the influence of randomness.
If the outcome differs from your opinion, you may feel invalidated or start questioning why your prediction was wrong.

Since immediate results are always influenced by randomness, thinking about them is pointless.
Just follow the pre-tested rules and keep trading according to them, win or lose.
What's important is how well you can let go of immediate results and understand that predicting them is not your job.

You often hear the advice "don't listen to others 'opinions," but you should also "not listen to your own opinion."
Your opinion only justifies your current emotions.
What you should listen to is not your opinion but the "rules."
Focus solely on what the rules say and keep acting accordingly.

Discipline and consistency are often emphasized in trading, but many people mistakenly believe that their own opinions are more valuable.
The common mistake people make is being consistent with their "opinions."
This means being consistent with their emotions because opinions only justify emotions.
Following emotions leads to actions like avoiding losses or stop losses and prematurely securing small profits from fear of losing them.
This means taking high risks for small rewards, continuously repeating a strategy with very poor risk-reward ratios, which guarantees failure.

Your opinion doesn't matter; what matters is the rule.
Some might feel their self-esteem is hurt by this, but trading should not be a battle between your ego and the chart.
Your reason for trading should simply be "because it's the rule."

Keep this in mind.

TRUE UNDERSTANDING OF A TRADER'S JOB IS THE KEY TO SOLVING ALL PROBLEMS

The solution to the problems you encounter in trading depends on how clearly you understand trading itself.
It's often said, "Trading is not a battle with the chart, but a battle with yourself."
Many interpret this as a battle with their emotions, but this is only a superficial understanding.
What it truly means is a battle with your lack of understanding and experience.
Emotions are not the cause but the result.
They reflect your lack of understanding, and battling your emotions won't lead to success in trading.
The fundamental solution lies in how deeply you understand trading.

As a trader, here is what you need to understand:
1. True understanding of a trader's job

2. Thorough backtesting of your system and acquiring the skills to verify and reproduce its edge
3. Understanding probabilistic thinking and embodying it in your actions
4. Understanding how probabilities work

I have reiterated this many times, but truly understanding these four points will fundamentally resolve emotional issues, eliminating the worry of taking inappropriate actions. Conversely, if you have any problems as a trader, they relate to one of these areas.
Analyze your issues well and consider what is lacking or what is unnecessary.
The battle with yourself is a battle with your lack of understanding.

From this perspective, if you can conquer the "battle with yourself," trading becomes a straightforward task of clicking.
In essence, trading is simply the repetitive execution of predetermined actions.
Your lack of understanding and incorrect perceptions about trading cause various problems.
It's not about controlling emotions but correcting the underlying false beliefs and thought processes through proper understanding.

ANXIETY AND FEAR

You cannot eliminate emotions entirely, but it is possible to adopt thought processes that prevent these emotions from arising in specific situations.
You feel anxiety and fear because you do not know something, it is unknown, or you think it may harm you.
If these reasons disappear, you will no longer feel fear.
This does not mean you have become an emotionless robot; rather, your thought process in that situation has changed.
Some people say, "Humans cannot become like robots," but they misunderstand the true meaning of not trading emotionally.
It's not about erasing all emotions but about ensuring you do not perceive your trading as something to fear.

Emotions are the result of your thought processes and serve as signals.
The first step is to become aware of your own anxiety and fear.
By recognizing your anxiety and fear, you can identify the thought processes triggering them.
Behind your emotions are thought processes, and emotions arise as automatic reactions based on specific triggers.

In a clear case, you might be muttering something to yourself when you feel these emotions.
"Why isn't it going up?" "The amount is now half of what it

was then!"
Think carefully about the beliefs behind these words.
The phrase "Why isn't it going up?" indicates beliefs like "My prediction should be correct," "The market is predictable," "Analytical skills mean the accuracy of predictions," and "A good trader never misses a prediction."
Understanding logically why these beliefs are wrong and what is correct, and accepting this through experience, can change these beliefs.
Thus, the emotions we experience are superficial layers of thought processes and beliefs, and recognizing emotions helps identify the triggers and beliefs causing them.

Start by becoming aware.
When you feel anxiety or fear, direct your attention to those emotions.
Next, focus on the internal dialogue in your mind.
Write these down in a trading journal.

Many people might find it difficult to become aware of emotions when overwhelmed by anxiety or fear.
Often, by the time you notice, you have already acted based on those emotions.
When emotions overwhelm us, we cannot think clearly.
This is why writing is essential.

Once you write down the emotions you noticed and the internal dialogue, you can slowly analyze them.
Don't try to do everything in your head at once.
This is like giving a high-load task to an already burdened computer.
It might feel cumbersome, but how you face yourself and what you think is crucial.

Approaching such an important task in the most effective way is key.

WHEN YOUR SYSTEM FAILS

Your system fails when you lose consistency, not when you incur losses, experience losing streaks, or go through drawdowns.

Losing streaks and drawdowns are part of the system and do not indicate a malfunction.
They signify that the system is functioning correctly.
Think about this carefully.
The reason an edge system eventually yields profits is that you follow the rules and take stop losses and losing streaks as they come.
If a system doesn't yield profits after consistently following the rules and taking stop losses, then it lacks an edge.
Both outcomes indicate that the system is functioning normally, and if the results surprise you, it means you failed to verify its performance beforehand.
You merely thought you understood the system based on a small sample size.

Results from 50 or 100 trades are very small numbers in terms of probability and do not accurately reflect a system's performance.
You will inevitably experience significant fluctuations as you

continue to trade.
However, these fluctuations are just the normal range of the system's performance that you might not have experienced in testing.
Due to randomness, you will inevitably experience fluctuations.
The importance of leveraging the law of large numbers to draw out a system's edge lies in using the property that probabilities converge over the long run, despite fluctuations.

If you feel your system is not performing as tested, it might be that your understanding of its performance is wrong, your testing was insufficient, or your execution is flawed.
Many traders first question the system or the market before doubting their execution.
With a genuinely well-tested system, the first doubt should be about yourself.

Many traders lament that the market has changed or that their system doesn't work, even though they can't maintain the same trading strategy for a year.
The real change is often not in the market but in their behavior and resolve.
You should reexamine your tendency to change behavior and decisions.
First, doubt yourself.
Many traders say, "Fight yourself, not the market," but few are willing to doubt themselves.

Consistency is a crucial skill and essential in trading.
Consistency is a problem within yourself.

THE GAME OF ACCUMULATION

The term "probability game" often leads to misunderstandings among traders, causing them to fail in consistently gathering sample sizes in their trading.
Today, I want to introduce the concept of the "game of accumulation."

Many traders misunderstand "probability game" to mean the probability of winning a single trade.
This misunderstanding leads them to play the game of short-term wins and losses instead of focusing on the long-term accumulation.
Trading, more accurately, is a game of accumulation over multiple trades.
It's about moving forward three steps, then back two, then forward four steps and back one, and so on.
To ultimately end up with a positive balance, you need a substantial sample size.

Let's explain backtesting from this perspective.
Some traders dismiss backtesting, saying it's useless because past patterns don't repeat.
However, backtesting is about testing the "effectiveness of accumulation" using patterns, probabilities, and money

management strategies.

In my trading, I use a multi-timeframe system.
I enter at the beginning of a trend in the lower time frame when a pullback is identified in the daily or 4-hour chart.
The backtest examines how capital evolves when combining the small stop losses in the lower time frame with the potential rewards if the trend propagates to higher time frames.

For example:
- A stop loss results in -1.
- A small move that doesn't propagate to the 4-hour trend results in 0-1.
- A trend that propagates to the 4-hour chart results in 2-5.
This is a very rough illustration, but it's how I perceive my trading.
As long as I keep rolling my dice, I'm not overly worried about my capital dwindling.

In essence, I'm not checking how to win the next single trade.
Instead, I'm testing whether a sequence of trades, incorporating money management strategies, will likely result in capital accumulation over a large sample size.
This understanding allows me to focus on repeating the same trades with a long-term perspective throughout the year, without being swayed by immediate results.
With the awareness that trading is a game of accumulation, I have no doubt that a substantial sample size is necessary for success.

Traders who abandon their systems early are still trapped in the win-lose game and fail to transition to a different game.
The key question to verify beforehand is whether your rules

enable accumulation over time.

Forget about the probability of winning the next trade for now.

What you should check is whether it's possible to accumulate capital over multiple trades.

It's not just about the win rate; you also need to consider money management strategies and develop a sense of making profits over multiple trades.

YOU ARE A BABY TRADER

It is often said, "Trading is not a battle with the chart, but a battle with yourself," but too many people misunderstand this.
Many people take this to mean "a battle with their own emotions" and think that "if they control their emotions, they will succeed in trading," but this is not the case.
Even if you control your emotions, you will not succeed in trading.

The true meaning of this is "a battle with your lack of understanding of trading."
Emotions are simply a reflection of your lack of understanding.
Emotions are not the cause; they are the result.

For example, emotions may arise from incorrect beliefs and thought processes, such as "overemphasizing immediate results," fear from inadequate understanding of risk management strategies leading to reckless position sizes, or anxiety from insufficient testing of your system, not knowing if you have an edge.
No matter how much you control your emotions, if you do not understand trading, your reckless actions will not change,

and it is impossible to succeed.
All of this is due to your lack of understanding.

The reason you take dangerous actions or do things you shouldn't is due to your lack of understanding.
You are like a newborn baby who has not learned anything yet.
Do babies take dangerous actions due to a lack of emotional control?
Do they try to touch fire out of curiosity, or cry loudly in a quiet movie theater without considering the people around them because of a lack of emotional control?
They take dangerous actions because they have not yet learned or do not know what will happen if they do.
The solution is to learn.

When you say it is a battle with yourself, it is important to recognize it as a battle to nurture the baby trader in you, to recognize and improve the actions and emotions that come from your lack of understanding.
Rather than just thinking about dealing with emotions, seeing it this way makes it easier to find specific solutions.
What understanding are you lacking?
What incorrect beliefs and thought processes remain?
What actions remain as habits due to them?
You should be able to think specifically.

ABOUT BORING TRADES

Trading is boring.
Profitable trading is boring.

The phrase "Trading is boring" expresses that proper trading has no excitement, and while this phrase is correct, it is just an expression.
It might be a bit dangerous if you keep saying "boring, boring" all the time while looking at the screen during actual trading or waiting for a trade.
It is a sign that you are seeking stimulation, whereas in reality, you should not even feel that it is boring.
If you think "boring" too much, it means you want to do something.
You internally feel that you need to do something.

Would you feel restless and say you are bored after brushing your teeth and waiting for the next time to brush?
You wouldn't think about brushing your teeth at all, would you?
It is the same feeling for me.
After finishing the necessary chart checks for trading, I calculate the time to check next, set an alarm, and completely forget about trading until then.

Even when holding a position, I leave the chart and forget about trading.
I don't even feel bored.

This is because, for me, trading only involves necessary processes, and I understand perfectly that I don't need to do or think about anything else, and it has become second nature.
I don't even think about opening the chart when it's unnecessary, and I forget about trading altogether.
I don't care about the results of trading, and I don't bother to check how much I won or lost.
It's meaningless to me, and it's not part of the process I need to follow.
Those things can be done a year later.
I don't care about short-term results.

Trading is boring when everything you need to do is decided.
This is correct as an expression, and I also say it.
However, if you are actually watching the screen all the time, waiting for something and saying "bored, bored" too much, you should be careful.
Check if you are unconsciously seeking stimulation.
If what you need to do is truly clear and staying in front of the chart is meaningless now, set chart alerts or time alarms and step away from the chart to do daily life activities.
You need an appropriate distance from trading, and when you eliminate everything outside the process, there is very little you actually need to do.
Enrich your daily life outside of trading.

CONSISTENCY IS THE PROOF OF BEING A TRADER

Consistency is not a matter of mindset; it is an undeniable skill.
Trading consistency goes beyond merely following rules; it encompasses your entire understanding of trading.

I was a disciplined person even before I started trading, yet I couldn't adhere to trading rules.
This involves instinctive reactions; when you have incorrect thought processes or understandings of trading, they trigger instinctive rejection responses that you cannot resist.
Even if you manage to resist once, trading is a very long process and an endless cycle.
If resisting once is so difficult, continuing on that long path is extremely challenging.

Truly excellent traders do not struggle with consistency.
This is because their fundamental approach to trading, their perception of winning and losing, their responsibilities, and what they need to do have all been replaced by a deep understanding of trading.

Creating a superior trading system is the first hurdle as a trader.
This is a challenge that many people can overcome if they put in the effort.
The problem comes after that, with the "consistency test."
This test assesses whether you have the proper mindset, adequate preparation, and the qualities of a trader by seeing if it can generate doubts and distrust in you.

This challenge is related to how many incorrect beliefs you still hold, how well you understand probabilistic thinking, how well you comprehend what you are doing, how much you trust statistics, whether you have tested with a sample size large enough to trust, and how many bad habits you can eliminate.
These are the exact challenges for us traders who trade with probabilistic thinking.

These are quite specific tasks.
If you perceive what I am saying as a matter of mindset or psychology, you may not be grasping the essence.
Don't just dismiss consistency as a matter of mindset or psychology; seriously engage with these tasks.
Think carefully about how well you are doing, what you need to do.
If you are truly struggling with the "consistency test," the final hurdle, you should understand what I am saying.

Understanding your job as a trader, the scope of your responsibilities, probabilistic thinking, how probabilities work, and why a reliable sample size is necessary all come together to form a trader's consistency.
For the parts you understand shallowly, reread the relevant

pages multiple times.
Then, translate them into your own specific tasks.

Misunderstanding "Coping with" and "Adapting to" the Market

Many people misunderstand what it means to "cope with" and "adapt to" the market.
Coping with and adapting to the market does not mean constantly changing your strategy or system to match the market's movements.

Many traders cannot consistently use the same system for even a few months, abandoning or tweaking it at the first sign of a losing streak or drawdown.
They say the market has changed in just a few months (or even shorter periods) and that their system is no longer working.
They think they need to cope with the changing market.

This perspective is too short-term.
Properly coping with the market means encompassing all market movements through a large sample size.

Probability does not stabilize with small sample sizes.

If you have only tested 100 times, the results are heavily influenced by randomness, and there is a range of variations you have not yet seen.
If you have only tested 100 times, different results in the next 100 trades might make you think "the market has changed" or "the system is no longer working."
This simply means that performance you have not seen yet is appearing.
However, if you backtest with 1,000 trades over 10 years and 10 currency pairs, the sample size increases to 10,000 trades, making probability stabilize and less susceptible to change.
This is the "law of large numbers," meaning that probabilities converge, and accurate performance can be understood through a large sample size.

Of course, this includes trending and non-trending markets, and systems with an edge are designed to leave profits even in less favorable market conditions through rules that avoid unfavorable situations as much as possible, along with appropriate profit-taking and stop-loss rules.
Therefore, coping with the market means dealing with it through a large sample size.

I use a trend-following strategy, but my system has been extensively tested over a long period, and it is designed to minimize participation in non-trending situations and to leave profits even with appropriate stop-losses when participating.
The market does not continue trending all the time, and the market naturally changes over short periods.
However, this is already factored into my strategy, and from the perspective of my span, nothing has changed.

Many traders change their systems frequently and cannot maintain consistency.
They should trade with the same system for several years before saying "the market has changed," and they should prepare thoroughly for this.
Excellent traders who maintain consistency over several years do not easily say "the market has changed" based on a few months or weeks of results because they have tested extensively with large sample sizes in advance.
They are not looking at such short periods.
It would take thousands or tens of thousands of trade samples to overturn their probabilistic performance, and a few losing streaks do not affect them.
Even during losing streaks, they continue trading according to the rules without hesitation.

Losing streaks and drawdowns are unavoidable.
Understand that they are part of the system.
Build enough trust through thorough preparation to handle this.
You are trying to use the laws of probability, and you need a large sample size.
Consistency is required.
Consistency includes all aspects of a trader's understanding.
Consistency is what makes a trader.

CAUSES OF REVENGE TRADING

- Thought processes that place value on winning and losing.
- Perceiving losses as bad.
- Not understanding that stop losses also have an edge.
- Self-esteem dependent on trading results.
- Feeling of defeat.
- Misunderstanding that the market can be controlled.
- Short-term perspective and the desire to feel good now above all else.
- Lack of self-discipline.
- Arrogance in thinking your judgment is better than the rules to be followed.
- Lack of understanding of a trader's job.
- Lack of trust and understanding in the system.
- Lack of understanding of the randomness of the market.
- Lack of understanding of the importance of risk management.
- Lack of or non-adherence to a trading plan.

You might think that the problem with revenge trading is the inability to control emotions, but the emotions themselves are caused by incorrect thinking and a lack of understanding. Before attributing everything to emotional control, you need to thoroughly understand the necessary thought processes and the trader's job.

If you understand how much revenge trading hinders your success and that it is an act of self-destruction as a trader, you will not willingly engage in it.

CHAPTER 3: Q&A AND CASE STUDIES

In this chapter, I will address common questions and concerns that traders often have, as well as frequently asked questions sent to me. Through this format, I will introduce how to approach and think about dealing with trading problems.

Q. HOW MANY CONSECUTIVE LOSSES SHOULD I TOLERATE?

A.
If you have an edge, you can tolerate any number of consecutive losses.

The number of consecutive losses you can tolerate is not a matter of your mental tolerance, but rather whether your system can maintain profitability.
First, let's clarify this as many people confuse the two.

If the system can maintain a positive balance, then you can tolerate any number of consecutive losses within that range.
This depends on the system's rules.
For example, if the trailing stop rule allows you to "protect the position quickly but reduce the win rate," the number of consecutive losses will increase, but the total loss amount may not increase significantly.
Even if the win rate drops, the amount of money lost is small.

Many traders misunderstand this too: a low win rate does not

mean losing a lot of money.
Due to the stop rules, it can mean small losses are controlled but the number of stop-outs increases.
Ultimately, it's about balancing total profit, so considering the number of consecutive losses is meaningless.

The important thing is not the number of consecutive losses but whether repeating the same trades multiple times leaves a profit.
Those concerned about consecutive losses are likely troubled by placing too much value on the immediate trading results from a short-term perspective.

Conduct thorough backtesting to confirm if profits remain.
If there is a profitable strategy, then the edge includes the consecutive losses that occur.
Those losses are generating the profits.
It's important not to resent the consecutive losses but to view them as part of the profit-generating process.
A long-term perspective and considering the system as a whole are crucial.

Q. WHY DON'T REAL TRADES YIELD THE SAME RESULTS AS BACKTESTS?

A.

If your real trades do not yield the same results as backtests, consider the following:

- How large was the sample size in your backtests?
- What sample size are you using to judge your real trades?
- Are you truly trading as per the backtest conditions?
- Did you manually conduct the backtests thoroughly?
- Did you avoid any form of cheating in your backtests?
- Did you consider news events in your backtests?

Many traders observe too short a period or refer to too small a sample size, making it difficult to accurately assess performance in both backtests and real trades.

It's possible that the performance of the system that you are unaware of is simply manifesting.

If you haven't conducted backtests with a large sample size, you might not yet know the exact performance and are just

surprised by the unknown parts.
If you have thoroughly conducted backtests with a large sample size (at least 1,000 times over a 10-year period), it would take a considerable sample size to overturn that performance, so the question is whether you are judging your real trades based on such a large sample size.
Many traders start doubting their system after just a few losing trades.
If you have truly tested with a large sample size, you will need an even larger sample size to overturn that system.

Before doubting the system, the first thing to doubt is your own actions.
Are you truly trading according to the rules?
Did you manually conduct the backtests thoroughly?
Did you use the rewind function to redo trades after seeing the results, thinking, "Oh, this fits the rules, so I'll count it"?
The important thing is whether you can read the signals from the chart before knowing the results.
Did you consider news events when conducting backtests?

Ask yourself these questions first.
Blaming the system or the market is easy, but if you have conducted backtests with a large sample size, the problem is most likely with yourself.

Q. IS IT REALLY OKAY FOR TRADING TO BE AS SIMPLE AND EASY AS JUST REPETITION?

A.
Simple and easy are different things.

If you think it is easy, you should try it.
You will understand that it is the most difficult thing in trading.

No matter how much of an edge your system has, continuously repeating it "no matter what happens" is very difficult.
To achieve the strong consistency required to not be affected by immediate results, losing streaks, or drawdowns, you must deeply understand the concept of utilizing probability and possess the qualities of a trader.

While the actions may seem like simple repetition, what hinders you is your own instincts.

If you have incorrect thought processes or beliefs, you will have to fight against strong internal resistance, and it is nearly impossible to win against yourself.
Even if you win once, trading requires you to repeat this forever, and I know no one who can maintain consistency with incorrect beliefs.
Despite the many traders around the world, almost all of them have found it impossible.
This is why trading is said to be "simple in repetition but the most difficult."

However, this simplicity is necessary to utilize probability.
You may think trading is simple because you only see the repetitive aspect.
What you must do to reach this point is not simple.
For example, finding an edge in the market and repeatedly testing and refining it is a difficult process.
Preparation is crucial in trading, and the "repetition" stage you perceive as simple and easy is actually the final stage of trading.
To truly make these processes simple and easy, you must identify and transform your beliefs and thought processes.

Ultimately, the tasks may become simple and easy, but the journey to reach that point is very difficult and time-consuming.
Understand this, and continue to face the world of trading seriously without underestimating it.

Q. I feel frustrated

after skipping an entry, only to see the trade move significantly in the direction I was planning to trade.

A.
Trading is not a game where you compete to see if your predictions are correct.

If you feel frustrated, your approach to trading is fundamentally wrong and very dangerous.
You are too involved in the outcome, placing too much value on winning and losing, having a short-term perspective, mistakenly believing that the market can be predicted, and not fully understanding probabilistic thinking for trading success.
You are making various misunderstandings and errors in thinking.

This is a common mistake among beginners and those new to trading.
You need to switch this mindset to probabilistic thinking

and understand that consistency and sample size determine success.
What matters is not individual wins and losses but how consistently you can repeat trades according to your rules.
You need to strictly adhere to the rules and take losses as necessary.
Your opinion does not matter.
Even if you think the market is not likely to go up, you must enter and take the stop-loss according to the rules.
You should not think, "It didn't go up as I thought, I shouldn't have entered."
Thinking like this makes it increasingly difficult to follow the rules, and eventually, you will prioritize your opinion over the rules, losing consistency.

No one knows the future of the market, nor do they need to.
Your job is to repeat the actions determined by your rules to utilize the laws of probability and extract the edge of the system.

You should not care whether the market moved as you predicted.
Consider your trade successful only if you acted according to the rules.
If you did not follow the rules, think carefully about why.
Within those reasons, you will find hints to solve the problems that compromise your consistency.

Q. DRAWDOWNS ARE TOUGH.

A.
Drawdowns are unavoidable. When you feel they are tough, write down what you are thinking.

No matter how excellent the system, losing streaks and drawdowns are unavoidable.
When you feel they are tough, there are specific thought processes or beliefs behind those feelings.
Write down what you are thinking.
You can identify the root of the problem.

If you are thinking, "What if the losses continue?", it may be because you have not built trust in the system, or you do not fully understand probabilistic thinking.
If you are thinking, "Maybe the system has stopped working," it might be because you are looking at too short a period or do not understand the law of large numbers.

Emotions arise based on what you are unconsciously thinking.
When emotions arise, look at the thoughts behind them to identify the cause.

If you have thoroughly backtested and built trust in your

system, understand probabilistic thinking, and are dedicated to your role, then "worrying about results" should be eliminated from your process.
Your process should only involve "waiting," "confirming," and "clicking."
Frequently checking charts without reason, counting losing streaks, or looking at the graph of your account balance during drawdowns are not part of your process.

Using a system in actual trading means doing it with such determination that there is no turning back.
Start with enough preparation to be able to commit to not changing anything for at least a year.
The only way to tackle inevitable drawdowns is by changing how you perceive trading.
You cannot eliminate drawdowns themselves.
If you can focus on the process with the determination to complete a full year, you will understand that drawdowns are just part of the journey, and though the road may not be smoothly paved, it is still the path to your destination.

Q. YOU SAY TO CONTINUE DESPITE LOSING STREAKS, BUT WHEN SHOULD I CONSIDER CHANGING THE SYSTEM?

A.

The time to consider changing or improving the system is during backtesting.

In real trading, doubt not the system but whether you are adhering to the rules, maintaining consistency, and questioning yourself.

Do not easily change a system that has been tested with a large sample size based on a small sample size in real trading.

Many people have too short an observation period and become anxious if their capital does not increase in just one month, leading them to tinker with or abandon the system.

If you have followed the rules perfectly, it is okay to continue for a year even if your capital decreases.
The problem is when you stop because you think, "If I continue like this, my capital will decrease in a year."
Many traders cannot continue for a year and have not confirmed in advance through backtesting that they will be profitable several times a year.
If you have thoroughly confirmed in advance that you will be profitable over the year, continue no matter how anxious you get along the way.
No one knows whether you will be in profit or loss a year later; you can consider that when it happens.
If you cannot maintain consistency due to anxiety about an unknown future, you will never be able to maintain consistency.
The day when the future is guaranteed will never come.
Therefore, you have no choice but to trust your thorough prior preparation and cannot quit halfway.

If you are so uncertain about your system, conduct even more thorough backtesting.
Performing it over ten thousand times will significantly reduce your anxiety, but have you done that?
If you want to become a professional, you must do what professionals do.
Conduct an enormous amount of backtesting that no one else does.

Q. HOW CAN I AVOID UNEXPECTED STOP LOSSES?

A.
You cannot predict any outcome.

Stop losses are unavoidable.
If you could anticipate them, you wouldn't enter the trade in the first place.
Both profits and stop losses are unexpected.
However, since you have a stop-loss rule in place, no matter how unreasonable the stop loss may seem, you can always limit the loss to a certain percentage.
This is risk management.

Understand that stop losses are inevitable and not inherently bad.
Do not try to find reasons for the loss.
In hindsight, anything can be explained, but it is impossible to accurately predict the future without knowing the results.
The reason for the stop loss does not matter.
What is important is to execute the predetermined stop-loss rule and consistently limit the loss to a certain percentage.
This way, every stop loss, regardless of the reason, becomes

just another stop loss.
Stop focusing on individual outcomes.

By always keeping losses within a certain limit, you are merely paying a fixed participation fee for a ticket that offers potential returns beyond the cost.

Unexpected stop losses cannot be avoided, and the results are always unexpected.
Accept that unexpected results will occur.
Consider trading as a game where you increase your capital by repeatedly experiencing both wins and losses, always prepared for inevitable losses.

Q. IS IT TRUE THAT NO STRATEGY WORKS FOREVER?

A.
Many traders misunderstand this phrase to mean "it will never work again in the future," but that is not what it means.

Using the trend-following strategy as an example, the phrase "no strategy works forever" means "trends do not last forever," which is obvious.
It is also obvious that this does not mean trends will never appear again in the future.
Trends will eventually appear again.

Traders who misunderstand this phrase to mean "it will never work again" interpret it as needing to constantly change strategies to match the market.
This approach cannot utilize probabilities effectively.
In probabilistic thinking, determining whether the market has changed requires a sample size, and taking countermeasures also requires a sample size.
As a result, the market will have changed again by the time the countermeasures are implemented, creating a perpetual catch-22 situation.

This is caused by looking at too short a period and misunderstanding the phrase "no strategy works forever."

A trend-following strategy can function through filtering rules and stop-loss rules that avoid trading when there are no trends.
The belief that "a stop-loss means the strategy is not working" is fundamentally wrong.
An edge-based system is designed so that when a trend finally occurs, the profits remain due to these stop-loss rules.
Therefore, stop-losses also have an edge, and the system is functioning correctly.
A longer-term perspective is necessary to understand this.
A good trend-following strategy creates an edge by assuming there will be periods with trends and without trends, and it operates on a long-term perspective with a large sample size.

Thinking from a longer-term perspective is important.

Strictly speaking, the exact same market never exists, and the market changes.
However, when considering a broader timeframe, there are only trends and ranges.
I have watched the market for over 15 years and have experienced various black swan events.
Each time, I have heard opinions that "the market has changed," but in reality, there are only trends and ranges, with different names and labels.

With excellent risk management rules and stop-loss rules, losses can always be limited to a certain percentage, making each stop-loss just another outcome.
For trend followers, a trending market brings significant profits.

This is trend-following.
If your trading is simply a numbers game or a probabilities game, then the reasons for individual losses are meaningless.
You are always paying a predetermined participation fee for a lottery ticket with the potential for a higher payout.
To truly play the probabilities game, a large sample size and long-term perspective are essential, and seeking meaning in individual outcomes or reasons is contradictory.
"There's no die that always wins" or "there's no die with a 100% win rate" are obvious statements, but this does not mean your capital will not increase.
Understand this well.

Q. It's tough even if I think that the immediate wins and losses don't matter.

A.
The belief that immediate wins and losses are important still remains.

Trying to convince yourself that immediate wins and losses don't matter won't eliminate old beliefs.
You need to experience and truly believe that they don't matter.

When I was a child, I was afraid of roller coasters.
In middle school, I didn't like that everyone else seemed to enjoy them while I was scared, so I practiced riding them.
Even though I understood intellectually that I wouldn't die, I was still scared.
But after riding the same roller coaster many times, my fear turned into confidence through experience.
Now, I have no fear of roller coasters and understand them as something fun.
This shows that beliefs won't change just by trying to convince yourself; they change through understanding gained from experience.

Many traders cling to the phrase "the results don't matter" to ease the pain of immediate wins and losses and try to convince themselves, but this doesn't change anything.
You need to experience it.
You need to experience many times that single results do not affect success at all.

Utilize backtesting more.
Backtesting is not just data collection.
You need to not only understand intellectually that a single stop-loss is not fatal but also experience it many times.
You need to experience repeatedly that in the end, there are profits left.
Often people say, "I've done enough backtesting," but if you are struggling with real trading, it's not enough.
When you feel "I've done enough backtesting," you are still at the starting line.
Even if you feel tired of doing the same thing over and over again, you need to continue doing it.

The monotony you gain from repetition and the sense of emptiness you overcome will carry over to real trading.
If you still feel nervous and excited in real trading, you haven't done enough backtesting yet.

Q. WHEN SHOULD I ADJUST MY SYSTEM DURING REAL TRADING?

A.
In real trading, you generally do not adjust your system.
All adjustments should be completed during the backtesting phase.

The results of backtesting conducted with a large sample size are reliable.
The reliability of statistical data and probabilities lies in the sample size.
The larger the sample size, the more the law of large numbers comes into play, making the system less susceptible to the influence of randomness.
A few losing streaks will not significantly affect the probability, reflecting the true performance of the system.
Conversely, with a small sample size of about 100 trials, performance can easily be affected by randomness and is thus unreliable.

If you have truly conducted backtesting with a large sample size, such as 10,000 times, you would understand that a losing streak of about 10 trades does not negate the performance of the system and would not feel the need to make any changes.
In fact, within those 10,000 tests, there must have been losing streaks of 10 trades.
These losing streaks are also part of the system.

Commit to not altering the system at all for one year before engaging in real trading.
If you feel the need to make changes within a year, you have not done enough backtesting.
You have not built trust in your system or understood how to utilize probabilities.

To utilize probabilities, you need to gather a large sample size.
Failing to maintain consistency will result in failure.
Maintaining consistency depends on how much you can trust your system and understand how to utilize probabilities.
Conduct thorough backtesting beforehand, and in real trading, maintain consistency "no matter what happens."
Keep this in mind.

Q. ISN'T BACKTESTING DANGEROUS BECAUSE IT ALLOWS FOR CURVE FITTING?

A.
It's not backtesting that is dangerous, but you who might curve fit that is dangerous.

Sometimes people say, "Backtesting is dangerous because of curve fitting," but that's not an issue with backtesting; it's an issue with you.
You're not conducting backtesting the right way.
If you use that logic, real trading without proper methods is even more dangerous, but would you stop real trading?

Many traders dislike backtesting and come up with various reasons, but nothing else allows you to efficiently collect a large sample size over a long period, find the edge of your system, and practice probabilistic thinking.
Some say forward testing is better, but each serves a different

purpose, and it's not about replacing one with the other; this claim is also off the mark.

To avoid curve fitting, do not use the rewind function in backtesting and always repeat trades according to pre-determined rules.
Tools are effective only when used correctly.
Using them correctly is your responsibility.
Stop blaming the tools because you can't use them properly.

Q. HOW CAN I AVOID OVERTRADING?

A.
Simply trade according to your rules.

If you follow your rules and end up trading 50 times in a day, that is not overtrading.
Overtrading refers to the extra trades that fall outside your rules.

Therefore, do not judge overtrading based solely on the number of trades.
Instead, confirm whether the trades you made adhered to your rules.
If you find yourself making extra trades outside of your rules, it indicates a lack of probabilistic thinking and shallow understanding.

To utilize probabilities, you need to repeatedly trade under the same conditions and gather a large sample of trades with those conditions.
If different conditions mix into your sample size, you won't be able to extract the true edge of your system.
Understand this well and maintain the mindset that you are not trading for immediate results.
If you grasp this concept well, you will adopt a long-term

perspective and avoid overtrading.
This is because your trading purpose will change.

Q. HOW IMPORTANT DO YOU THINK INTUITION IS IN TRADING?

A.
Intuition is unnecessary.

You can only extract the edge of your system by consistently following its rules.
Using your system's edge is not about winning this one trade in front of you.
You must keep repeating the trades regardless of whether you win or lose.
The edge is extracted when probabilities function over the collected sample size.

If you prioritize intuition over the system's rules, it is no longer the same system.
If you must use intuition, then translate that intuition into repeatable rules that can be consistently applied.
Without repeatability, it becomes mere whims and moods, which cannot hold a probabilistic edge.

Stop thinking, "I would have won if I had followed my intuition."
That one outcome is random, and you might have lost as well.
In that case, you would feel, "I'm glad I followed the rules and was saved."
You should not judge the correctness of a trade based on one random outcome.

Just as you shouldn't trade based on others 'opinions, you also shouldn't trade based on your own opinions.
You should follow the system's rules that have been statistically proven to have an edge, not your own opinions.

Q. I'm too busy with work to find time for backtesting.

A.
Then stop real trading until you have time for backtesting.

Trading without backtesting is gambling.
How can you trade without knowing if your strategy has an edge or without clearly defined rules?
You fundamentally do not understand trading.
You do not understand the job of a trader.

The first step is to have a system with an edge supported by statistics from a large sample size.

Without this, you can't do anything.
Would you enter an operating room and perform surgery as an amateur without studying or practicing because you are too busy with work?
That would be unthinkable.
Trading is easy to start for anyone, so it's easy to misunderstand, but participating in the market without a strategy with an edge and without practice is suicidal.

It may sound harsh, but it is not me who is harsh, it is the market.
The market is not kind enough to make you rich with such naive thinking.
In fact, I am saying this out of kindness for you.
If you can't find time for backtesting, then stop trading.
I have seen many people ruin their lives by underestimating the market.
Please resume only after you have prepared thoroughly.
This is for the sake of your life.

Q. WHAT PERCENTAGE SHOULD I SET AS MY DAILY PROFIT TARGET?

A.
You should not set a profit target.

Profits depend on the market and are beyond your control.
Setting goals based on what you can't control leads to unnecessary self-criticism and misguided attempts to find reasons for outcomes, which undermines consistency.

The only goal you should set is whether you followed your rules.
If you adhered to your rules, it doesn't matter if the day ended in a loss or even if you didn't trade at all.

Do not have expectations of the market.
The market is governed by randomness and cannot be controlled by us.
Finding certainty within this uncertainty is the essence of

probabilistic thinking, and trading based on this is crucial. For this, you need a system with an edge and must consistently follow your rules over the long term.

Your goal is to stick to your rules throughout the day.

Q. HOW DO YOU INCORPORATE NEWS AND EVENT RISKS INTO YOUR STRATEGY?

A.
For foreseeable events, I establish rules in advance.

I have a rule that if there is no entry opportunity until a few hours before the announcement of significant economic indicators or news events, I do not take any new entries.

This rule is related to my trailing stop rule.
In the case of a buy entry, my trailing stop rule states that the trailing stop is raised to the new low when the chart confirms a higher high and higher low.
This is based on Dow Theory, but it takes about 6-8 candlesticks to clearly see this.
If trading on the hourly chart, that's 6-8 hours.
If trading on the 15-minute chart, that's 2 hours.
Therefore, when trading on the hourly chart, I do not take

new entries within 8 hours before significant events.
This creates the possibility of protecting the position with a trailing stop before the event, and even if the trailing stop is not triggered, there are two 4-hour candlesticks' worth of movement before the event, allowing me to close half the position before the event.

Thus, when facing an event while holding a position, I either have the position protected by a trailing stop or have reduced the position by half, thereby meeting the event with reduced risk.
This is made possible by the pre-set time rules for new positions before events based on my trailing stop rules.

Of course, these rules are strictly followed during backtesting, and I understand the system's performance with these rules applied. (For this reason, it is preferable to use backtesting software that also displays news events.)

I handle foreseeable events with these types of rules, but this is based on my trailing stop rule, so consider your own trading system when thinking about this.

There is no way to deal with unforeseeable sudden news events, so if I hold a position and it goes against me, I will take a loss.
This means the stop-loss is functioning correctly, so there is no problem.
That's what stop-losses are for in such situations, so avoid getting emotional or blaming sudden news events.

Q. HOW DO YOU MANAGE DRAWDOWNS?

A.
The only thing you can do during a drawdown is to stick to your rules.

No matter how good a system is, drawdowns are unavoidable. Trying to avoid the unavoidable will negate the system, and the edge will not be realized.

It is essential to assume that drawdowns will happen and prepare for them in advance.
This involves thorough backtesting to identify the maximum possible losing streaks and drawdowns from a large sample size of data and set position sizes accordingly.
Therefore, the only way to deal with drawdowns is to never deviate from the rules, which means "never do anything extra."

Consistency is crucial to extracting the edge of a system, and you must follow the rules no matter what happens.
Losses and losing streaks are inevitable.
Many traders deviate from the rules because of these, often

believing they are "improving" the system.
This is a mistake.
If you have thoroughly tested your system beforehand, trust the statistics and the edge.
Losses, losing streaks, and drawdowns are all part of the system.

Anyone can maintain consistency when their capital is steadily increasing.
Your true consistency is tested during losses, losing streaks, and drawdowns.
This consistency is built by "how thoroughly you prepared in advance," "how much trust you have in the system," and "how deeply you understand the job of a trader."

If you feel the need to do something during a drawdown or can't accept the drawdown, it means you haven't fully accepted the system yet.
Conduct even more thorough backtesting.
When you feel you have done "enough," consider that point as still before the starting line.
It is crucial to trust the system so much that you don't mind drawdowns or losing streaks and can accept them all.

Q. HOW SHOULD I ADJUST POSITION SIZES IN HIGHLY VOLATILE MARKETS?

A.
Always calculate your position size based on the stop-loss distance.

The determination of position size should always be based on the stop-loss distance.
No matter how high the volatility, calculate your position size according to the risk (percentage) set for that trade, based on the stop-loss distance.
However, in highly volatile situations, there may often be nearby resistance lines or unfavorable risk-reward ratios for taking profits, in which case rules to skip such trades are also necessary.
Decide in advance what is best based on statistical data from backtesting.

Q. How much backtesting should I do?

A.
Continue doing it every day for years.

The purpose of backtesting is not just data collection.
It serves as essential practice, much like it does for professionals in other fields.
This question is similar to asking a professional baseball player, "How long should you practice?" The answer is, "You continue practicing indefinitely."

I have been trading for 16 years. As a student, I would print out charts and manually backtest them during classes.
As an adult, I continued backtesting daily for years.
I considered backtesting to be necessary practice.
I backtested six currency pairs over ten years of data.
Once I completed all the data, I would repeat the same period over and over.
Repetition is essential for practice.
Even completing ten years of data for six currency pairs takes a considerable amount of time, and repeating this process takes years.
But as practice, it never ends.

I likely rank among the top in the world in terms of backtesting, and it has never let me down.
People often complain that real trading doesn't match backtesting results, but to me, it seems they have not done nearly enough backtesting.
Because they haven't backtested enough, they are unaware of their system's true performance and complain, "It doesn't match the backtesting results."
And if they had truly done extensive backtesting, they wouldn't be anxious over such a small sample size of real

trading and wouldn't hastily conclude that it doesn't match the backtesting results.
Ask yourself if you are trading exactly as you did during backtesting.
Without sufficient practice through backtesting, you might not be trading according to your backtesting results.

In other words, backtesting never ends.
Just as professionals in other fields don't declare their practice complete, traders should always value practice.

Backtesting solves all trading problems.
It helps create systems with an edge, builds statistical reliability, improves your trading skills and consistency, hones the ability to identify and execute signals from charts, and embodies probabilistic thinking.
As practice, doing it thoroughly for just a month is not enough.
Commit to doing it every day for years with serious intent.

In a few years, you will become an excellent trader.

Q. HOW SHOULD YOU TRADE IN DIFFICULT MARKETS?

A.
You shouldn't trade in difficult markets.

Skilled traders only trade in clear markets that align well with their trading rules.
Being a good trader is not about using every possible technique to make a profit in difficult markets.
The skill of a good trader lies in recognizing difficult markets and deciding not to trade, only engaging in trades when the situation clearly fits their rules.

Difficult or unclear markets are challenging for other traders as well, so orders are less likely to concentrate, making technical analysis less effective.
In clear markets, stop-loss orders and new orders tend to concentrate in the same areas, making technical analysis more effective.

Your job is not to make a profit on the trade in front of you.
It is to consistently follow the predetermined rules.
Wait patiently for situations that clearly match your rules and

only trade in those scenarios repeatedly.

Q. I can't make money because I have little capital.

A.
The reason you can't make money is the lack of an edge and consistency.

Many people lament that they can't make money because they have little capital, but the true reasons are the lack of an edge and consistency.
Other issues stem from these two fundamental problems.
Even if you had a lot of money, you would lose it all without the necessary skills.

It is true that with little capital, the amount you can earn from a single trade is small.
However, your job is not to make money from a single trade.
You need to consistently repeat the same trade to apply the law of large numbers and extract the edge, using the power of compound interest to grow your capital.

You need to think in long terms of 1 year, 2 years, 5 years, and 10 years.
Even if you make just 5% profit per month, that amounts to 60% in a year.

Repeating a 60% increase in capital over five years leads to astonishing amounts of money.
This is the power of compound interest.

There are no other professions where you can see such limitless salary increases over a few years.
This is why you should take trading seriously.
It is worth dedicating years to this profession.
It's not about becoming a millionaire from a single trade, although many people misunderstand and dream of this.
With time, it is possible and a career with potential.

Don't focus on how much you earn from a single trade.
Concentrate on building a system with an edge and maintaining consistency.
Trading is a world where you can earn unlimited money if you have the skills.
However, to achieve this, you need to forget about the money for a while.
How much you have now and how much you earn now are unrelated to your trading skills.

What you need is an edge and consistency.
The money will follow.

CONCLUSION

Thank you for reading to the end.
The necessary understanding for a trader is simple, but many traders focus on immediate results, fighting randomness, and fail to address what they should truly be doing as traders.
I hope that by reading this book to the end, you now have a clear understanding of what you should do as a trader.
What traders need is not to win the trade in front of them but to consistently prepare well in advance and operate a system with an edge.
I have tried to repeatedly explain this necessary understanding throughout this book.
Building a system with an edge is the first hurdle, but the real journey as a trader begins with consistently operating those systems.
Consistency is what makes a trader, and the journey to achieve consistency is the journey of trading.
I hope this book serves as a guidebook for your journey as a trader.
Please read this book repeatedly to deepen your necessary understanding as a trader.

I share information about trading daily on X.
My account is (@samuraipips358).
If you enjoyed the content of this book, please check out my daily posts.

They will surely be helpful for your trading.

I wish you a wonderful journey as a trader.
Thank you again for reading to the end.

Printed in Great Britain
by Amazon

52745736R00117